Michael George Mulhall

History of prices since the year 1850

Michael George Mulhall

History of prices since the year 1850

ISBN/EAN: 9783744739665

Printed in Europe, USA, Canada, Australia, Japan

Cover: Foto ©ninafisch / pixelio.de

More available books at **www.hansebooks.com**

HISTORY OF PRICES

SINCE THE YEAR 1850

BY

MICHAEL G. MULHALL,

FELLOW OF THE STATISTICAL SOCIETY AND OF THE SOCIETY OF ARTS;
HONORARY MEMBER OF THE SCOTTISH GEOGRAPHICAL SOCIETY;

AUTHOR OF

"THE DICTIONARY OF STATISTICS," "THE PROGRESS OF THE WORLD,"
"THE BALANCE-SHEET OF THE WORLD," ETC. ETC.

With Eight Coloured Diagrams

LONDON
LONGMANS, GREEN, AND CO.
1885

[All Rights reserved]

PREFACE.

Thirty years have elapsed since the last issue of Tooke and Newmarch's "History of Prices," and the interval has been one of the greatest commercial activity. It may appear surprising that so long a period has been allowed to pass without a review of the trade of nations in connection with the rise and fall of prices, but the magnitude of the undertaking has possibly deterred many competent persons. The utility of such a work, for the sake of reference, is beyond all question, and it only remains for the public to decide whether the task has fallen into proper hands.

MICHAEL G. MULHALL.

19 Albion Street, Hyde Park,
September 24, 1885.

NOTE.

Great Britain stands for United Kingdom, Austria for Austro-Hungary, and Scandinavia for Denmark, Sweden, and Norway.

The price of silver has fallen while the sheets were going through press, being now 47½ pence, instead of 49, as on page 12.

DIAGRAMS.

Price-level of Great Britain and the World	*Frontispiece.*
Stock of Gold and Silver	to face page 11
Taxation and Debt	,, ,, 30
Ocean Carrying-trade	,, ,, 35
Labour and Energy	,, ,, 55
Price-levels of Agriculture and Manufactures (the World)	,, ,, 122
Price-level of the World for one hundred years	,, ,, 130
Price-level of Great Britain, 1840–84	,, ,, 154

CONTENTS.

CHAPTER	PAGE
I.—Variations of price-level in Great Britain—Retrospect since 1850—Altered value of money	1–5
II.—Price-levels in Europe and America—Use and abuse of index numbers—Volume of trade method	6–10
III.—The precious metals—Stocks of gold and silver—Coinage of all nations—Price of silver	11–18
IV.—The money-market—Rates of discount—Banking in Great Britain and the Continent—Bankruptcy returns	19–25
V.—Finances of nations—Military expenditure—Public debts—Assets and liabilities of nations	26–32
VI.—Commerce of the world since 1850—Value and weight of sea-borne merchandise—Balance of trade—Import-dues—Trade of Great Britain	33–40
VII.—Shipping of all flags—Increase of steamers—Decline of American and French shipping—Effect of bounties	41–46
VIII.—Railways of the world—Capital invested therein—Freight and passenger tariffs—British railways—Telegraphs	47–51
IX.—Steam-power of the world—Work done by hand, horse, and steam—Cost of industry—Increase of energy in thirty-five years	52–57
X.—Textile manufactures—Consumption of cotton, wool, flax, jute—Value of goods manufactured	58–63
XI.—Iron and steel—Timber and forests of the world—Leather industry—Books and newspapers	64–70
XII.—Mining industry—California and Australia—Coal yield of the world—Various minerals	71–77

CHAPTER		PAGE
XIII.	Agriculture, area under crops, summary of grain-growing—Cattle-farming—Agricultural capital and product	78–85
XIV.	Food-supply of nations—Sum expended; amount of energy in food; meat-supply of Europe—Annual consumption of food per inhabitant in all countries	86–95
XV.	Population: increase in one generation—Decline of rural—Death-rate and days of sickness	96–100
XVI.	Emigration from Europe—Settlers in United States—Rise of the British Colonies—Colonial trade and finances	101–106
XVII.	Wealth and earnings of nations—Distribution of wealth in the United Kingdom—Cost of living in various countries	107–114
XVIII.	Summary of industries; numbers employed	115–116
XIX.	General survey of prices—Table of values from 1840 to 1884—Agriculture and manufactures	117–123
XX.	Wages in all countries; compared with cost of food, and with value produced	124–129
XXI.	One hundred years of wages and prices	130–133
XXII.	Causes that affect prices—Popular delusions in connection with prices	134–138
XXIII.	Review of British trade—Years of highest and of lowest prices—Effects of trade on wealth	139–143
XXIV.	Chronicle of events since 1850	144–152

APPENDIX.

Price-levels—Gold and silver—Banking and finances—Commerce and shipping—Railways—Manufactures—Agriculture and food-supply—Co-operative societies—Prices and index numbers—Writers on prices . . . 153–190

INDEX . . . 191

ERRATA.

Page 81, *line* 15, *for* 16 *read* 160.
Page 81, *line* 16, *for* 15 *read* 156.
Page 81, *line* 17, *for* 14 *read* 148.

Page 173. In Cattle Table (1880-1884) read as follows :—

	000's omitted.			
	Cows.	Horses.	Sheep.	Pigs.
United Kingdom	10,423	2,905	29,377	3,906
France	11,450	2,850	22,520	,570
Germany	15,790	3,520	19,190	9,210
Russia	27,320	17,590	51,820	10,840
Austria	13,180	3,280	13,100	7,160
Italy	4,780	658	8,600	1,160
Holland	1,430	270	750	400
Belgium	1,380	270	370	640
Denmark	1,470	350	1,550	530

HISTORY OF PRICES
SINCE THE YEAR 1850.

I.

VARIATIONS OF PRICE-LEVEL IN GREAT BRITAIN.

In reviewing the relations between gold and merchandise for a given term of years, the first thing is to ascertain the variations in value, not of one or two commodities, but of gold, and for this purpose it has been customary to adopt index numbers, an uncertain and deceptive method. Newmarch was sensible of this when he said, "Index numbers are open to the grave objection that raw silk is allowed the same importance as wheat." We have, however, an unerring guide at our command by comparing the actual total of trade with the sums which the same volume of merchandise would have amounted to at previous periods according to the prices then ruling.

Let us compare, for instance, the price-levels for Great Britain and the world since 1841-50 as follows:—

	Value in millions £		Price-level.	
At prices of	British trade of 1881-84.	Products of world, 1881-84	Great Britain.	World.
1841–50	704	5,186	100·0	100·0
1851–60	733	5,429	104·1	104·7
1861–70	877	5,762	124·6	111·1
1871–80	743	5,479	105·5	105·7
1881–84	644	4,910	91·5	94·7

We see that the variations in Great Britain have been greater than in the world at large. The price-level of the world for the years 1881–84 is about 15 per cent. lower than it was in the decade ending 1870—that is, 17 shillings will now buy as much as 20 shillings would then have done. Far from deploring this lower scale of prices, we must regard it as a great blessing, the result of improved machinery, cheaper cost of production, and economy in freight. Nor has it occasioned any loss to Great Britain, for the detailed tables in Appendix show that the price-level of our imports in 1881–84 is 30 per cent. less than in 1861–70, whereas that of our exports has fallen only 25 per cent. ; and as we import much more than we export, the difference of price-level is a gain to this country. No wonder, therefore, that although prices have declined, the volume of our trade expands and the public wealth increases.

The price-level in Great Britain, imports and exports together, showed a steady rise from 1850 to 1864, reaching a maximum of 152 in the latter year, and then declining almost continuously till the present, the level for 1884 being 13 per cent. below 1841–50. In a word, £87 will now buy as much in England as £152 in 1864, or £100 in 1841–50. If we take for standard the level of 1841–50, and compare the amounts of trade, according to custom-house returns, with what they would have been had prices not changed, we find as follows :—

Years.	Annual average, millions £		Ratio.	
	Scale of 1841–50.	B. of Trade returns.	Scale of 1841–50.	Board of Trade.
1851–60	244	254	100	104·1
1861–70	350	436	100	124·6
1871–80	562	592	100	105·5
1881–84	704	644	100	91 5

The first decade, showing a rise of 4 per cent., was a period of excitement and stirring events, such as the gold discovery in Australia, the Napoleon restoration in France, the Crimean war, the Indian mutiny, the crisis of 1857, the Franco-Lombard campaign, the Cobden treaty with France, &c., which affected in one or other way many branches of industry. Such was the tide of emigration that during the decade no fewer than 2,100,000 British subjects left our shores for America and Australia, say 8 per cent. of our population, which had a sensible effect on the labour market. The Crimean war caused a rise in flax, tallow, lead, and iron. Even wheat rose in spite of the repeal of the Corn Laws, the average price for the decade being 82 pence per bushel, or $2\frac{1}{2}$ per cent. over that of 1841-50. Meat, butter, and eggs likewise rose, the consumption having begun to outstrip the productive power of the country. In 1857 the price-level rose to 111, the nominal value of trade reaching 310 millions, though it should not have exceeded 279 millions, at prices of 1841-50. The same year is memorable for the great crisis in the United States, where 7,200 houses failed for an aggregate of 110 millions sterling, which had its repercussion in this country, bank-rate going up to 10 per cent., and the bullion reserve of the Bank of England falling to $6\frac{1}{2}$ millions.

The second decade opened with the war in the United States, which was for an interval disastrous to the interests of mankind, causing the greatest convulsion to trade that had been felt since the time of Buonaparté. Just before the close of the war, as already mentioned, prices in England reached an unprecedented level, and this was the immediate cause of the rage for Joint-Stock Limited Companies, of which three hundred sprung up in a year. Then came the Overend Gurney crisis in 1866, when no less than 100 millions were wiped off as bad debts in one short week, the Bank Act being again suspended (as in 1857), and the rate of discount again rising to 10 per cent. The same year saw the battle of Sadowa, the cattle-plague, stoppage of specie payments in Italy, and the Alabama claims, events all of a disturbing nature, and calculated to keep up the level of prices. Better days seemed dawning upon Europe with the completion of the Suez Canal in 1869, but were soon overclouded by the Franco-German war. Notwithstanding the cotton-famine, when this staple rose to five times its ordinary value, and the cattle plague carrying off 30,000 animals monthly, the decade was one of signal prosperity for Great Britain; the number of savings-banks depositors increasing by 800,000, and the wealth accumulations averaging 140 millions yearly. Much of this was due to Free Trade, the Cobden treaty of 1860 having given an impulse to international commerce all over Europe, to such a degree that the merchant navy of Great Britain (see Appendix) rose 77 per cent.

The third decade began under favourable auspices, with the conclusion of the Franco-German war, the opening of Mont Cenis tunnel, and the settlement of the Alabama claims; but trade was before long disturbed by a continuance of "strikes" in England and on the Continent, followed by an outbreak of war between Russia and Turkey, which reactionary causes for a time checked the beneficent fall in prices that mechanical improvements and cheapened transport were destined to bring about. During this decade the Suez Canal, after deducting fees, caused a saving of 20 millions sterling to the commerce of the world, a sum in excess of the total cost of its construction. Prices in Great Britain, especially for food, continued to rise, notwithstanding a fall in wheat, the average for which (1871–80) was 71 pence per bushel, the lowest rate known for so long a period since the time of George II. The decade was, moreover, remarkable for an abundance of capital, no less than 2,000 millions sterling (a large portion of it from England) having been devoted since 1871 to the construction of railways, besides 800 millions in new loans to various nations.

VARIATIONS OF PRICE-LEVEL IN BRITAIN. 5

The fourth period, comprising the years 1881–84, is by many people regarded as disastrous to British industry. It is true that the price average is 13 per cent. lower than in the decade ending 1880; but trade will quickly find its level, as it has so often done before: it would be monstrous if prices remained the same in spite of cheapened transport, improved machinery, and all the efforts of scientific progress. Until reasonable men become convinced that low prices are best, the teachings of economy will be in vain; but it ought to require little demonstration that if wool, raw cotton, coal and iron are cheaper, the manufacturer can afford to sell his wares for less than formerly.

Let us recapitulate the points of this chapter.

First. That 20 shillings will now buy as much of the world's products as 21 in the decade ending 1850.

Secondly. That the American war of 1862–65 drove up prices in Great Britain to an extravagant level.

Thirdly. That in the present depression of prices, as regards Great Britain, we find a greater decline since 1870 in the price-level of imports than of exports, and hence that Great Britain must be a gainer, seeing that our imports largely exceed our exports.

II.

PRICE-LEVELS IN EUROPE AND AMERICA.

WE have no detailed returns for each particular item of trade in foreign countries previously to 1860-62, but if we take those years as a basis for comparison, and adopt the method already alluded to (see Appendix) the price-levels of the principal countries will be found as follows:—

Years.	Gt. Britain.	France.	Italy.	Belgium.	U. S.	Medium.
1860-62	100	100	100	100	100	100
1863-70	118	94	103	90	114	104
1871-80	96	82	104	97	99	96
1881-83	85	75	82	85	94	84

The price-level of Europe reached its highest (115) in the year 1864, but the maximum for the world was in 1866, when the ratio stood at 123: the American war had recently terminated and the price-level of the United States gone up to 210 in greenbacks, or 170 in gold, the latter being the figure used in the above computations. The price-level for the world was again very high in 1872, after the Franco-German war. Hence it would seem that immediately after a war there is a demand for all kinds of merchandise in excess of supply, which causes prices to run up.

It may be said that £4 now will buy as much as £6 in 1866, the fall of prices being about 30 per cent., but as regards the United States in particular, we find a fall of 46 per cent., namely from 170 to 91, which is greater than has occurred in any other country; the extremes show a difference of 34 per cent. in France, 37 per cent. in Italy, and 43 per cent. in Great Britain.

PRICE-LEVELS IN EUROPE AND AMERICA.

Various economists and statists have endeavoured, from time to time, to lay down price-levels; constructed after different methods, they diverge considerably, but it is interesting to place them side by side:—

Years.	Soetbeer.	Jevons.	Laspeyre.	"Economist."	Mulhall	Medium.
1845–50	100	100	100	100	100	100
1851–55	114	107	111	...	104	109
1856–60	125	120	122	127	105	120
1861–65	127	123	123	...	110	121
1866–70	125	121	...	140	111	124
1871–75	136	...	...	127	112	125
1876–80	127	...	...	115	99	114
1881–84	124	...	...	105	92	107

All except mine have been based on index numbers, the fallacy of which it is important to demonstrate; if they were a correct guide we should conclude that the price-level of 1881–84 was higher than that of 1845–50, whereas the reverse was the case. That they have a certain attraction is undeniable, for Newmarch himself used them, while admitting their dubious character, but whenever used, the fewer the better, for if saltpetre and indigo be admitted on a footing with wheat, coal, and iron, the result must be erroneous. Jevons used 50, and the "Economist" 22, but the number should never exceed 10, and even then the result should be accepted with reserve.

Take, for example, ten principal items of trade in the United States (prices reduced to gold) which give us the following index numbers:—

	1841–50.	1851–60.	1861–70.	1871–80.	1881–83.
Butter	100	145	171	168	145
Cheese	100	135	158	180	180
Coal	100	100	104	76	72
Coffee	100	133	197	214	133
Cotton	100	126	436	169	133
Iron	100	91	91	98	57
Pork	100	109	100	100	156
Sugar	100	100	134	114	63
Tobacco	100	159	215	148	144
Wheat	100	136	129	112	102
Total	1,000	1,234	1,735	1,379	1,185

When we compare the above result with what is obtained by my method, which may be termed "the volume of trade," we see how remarkable is the difference and how deceptive index numbers may be :—

		Ratio.	
Years.	Index Numbers.	Index.	Trade.
1861–70	1,735	100	100
1871–80	1,379	80	89
1881–83	1,185	68	84

If the index numbers spoke correctly there must have been a fall of 32 per cent. in price-level, whereas anyone who takes the trouble to examine will find that the quantities of merchandise which passed through the American custom-houses in 1881–84 would have cost only 16 per cent. less than the same quantities in 1861–70. The following table shows (in gold) the actual amount of trade, and what it would have been if the average of prices in 1861–70 had remained unchanged :—

	Annual average, millions £.		Ratio.	
Years.	Scale of 1861–70.	Trade Returns.	Scale of 1861–70.	Trade Returns.
1861–70	92	92	100	100
1871–80	245	218	100	89
1881–83	378	317	100	84

That is to say, so far from £68 sufficing in 1881–83 to buy the same quantity of merchandise as £100 in 1861–70, it would have required £84 : this is a difference of such extreme importance that it calls for no further comment.

If we try the index numbers for ten principal articles of French trade we find as follows, according to the Customs valuation :—

PRICE-LEVELS IN EUROPE AND AMERICA.

	1861–70.	1871–80.	1881–83.
Cheese and butter	100	89	102
Coffee	100	105	84
Flax	100	67	45
Fruit	100	115	102
Grain	100	111	93
Meat	100	107	120
Silk	100	86	70
Sugar	100	106	95
Wine	100	81	105
Wool	100	88	79
Total	1,000	955	895

Here there is a decline of only 10½ per cent. from the level of 1861–70, whereas we find from the volume of trade method a fall of 21 per cent. in prices, viz. :—

	Annual average, millions £.		Ratio.	
Years.	Scale of 1861–70.	Trade Returns.	Scale of 1861–70.	Trade Returns.
1861–70	207	207	100	100
1871–80	344	296	100	86
1881–83	432	342	100	79

It is worth notice that whereas index numbers in the case of the United States made the fall of price appear double what it was in reality, the contrary has happened in the case of France, since we find from the trade volume method that the 20-franc gold piece will now buy as much as 25 francs in 1861–70, although the index numbers show a difference of value not exceeding 2½ francs in the same interval. Index numbers do not even err in a given direction, so that it is practically impossible to correct their uncertainties.

Finally, let us take the index numbers of ten principal articles of British trade, and see what they will give us :—

	1841-50.	1851-60.	1861-70.	1871-80.	1881-84.
Beef	100	110	119	143	167
Butter	100	101	129	136	126
Coal	100	112	125	150	112
Cotton	100	140	333	150	132
Flax	100	131	157	140	114
Iron	100	97	86	109	77
Sugar	100	94	100	79	58
Timber	100	79	79	70	64
Wheat	100	102	98	89	73
Wool	100	91	78	61	52
Total	1,000	1,057	1,304	1,127	975

If these index numbers were the real measure of value, we should find that prices in 1881-84 were only 2½ per cent. below the standard of 1841-50. We find, however, by the volume of trade method, that £91½ in 1881-84 would buy the same quantity of merchandise as £100 in the decade alluded to, and therefore the fall of price is 8½ per cent. The two systems, placed side by side, show as follows :—

Years.	Index Numbers.	Trade Volume.
1841-50	100·0	100·0
1851-60	105·7	104·1
1861-70	130·4	124·6
1871-80	112·7	105·5
1881-84	97·5	91·5

It is needless to proceed further in showing how unreliable is the system of index numbers, which will certainly be discarded before long by all economists and statists. On the other hand, nothing can be more certain than the volume of trade method, which has only the one drawback, that it involves a great amount of labour, but it is labour well requited, for we know that we have the exact measure of the rise or fall in the purchasing power of gold, instead of vague and illusory approximations, mere *ignes fatui*, that lead to the most deplorable pitfalls.

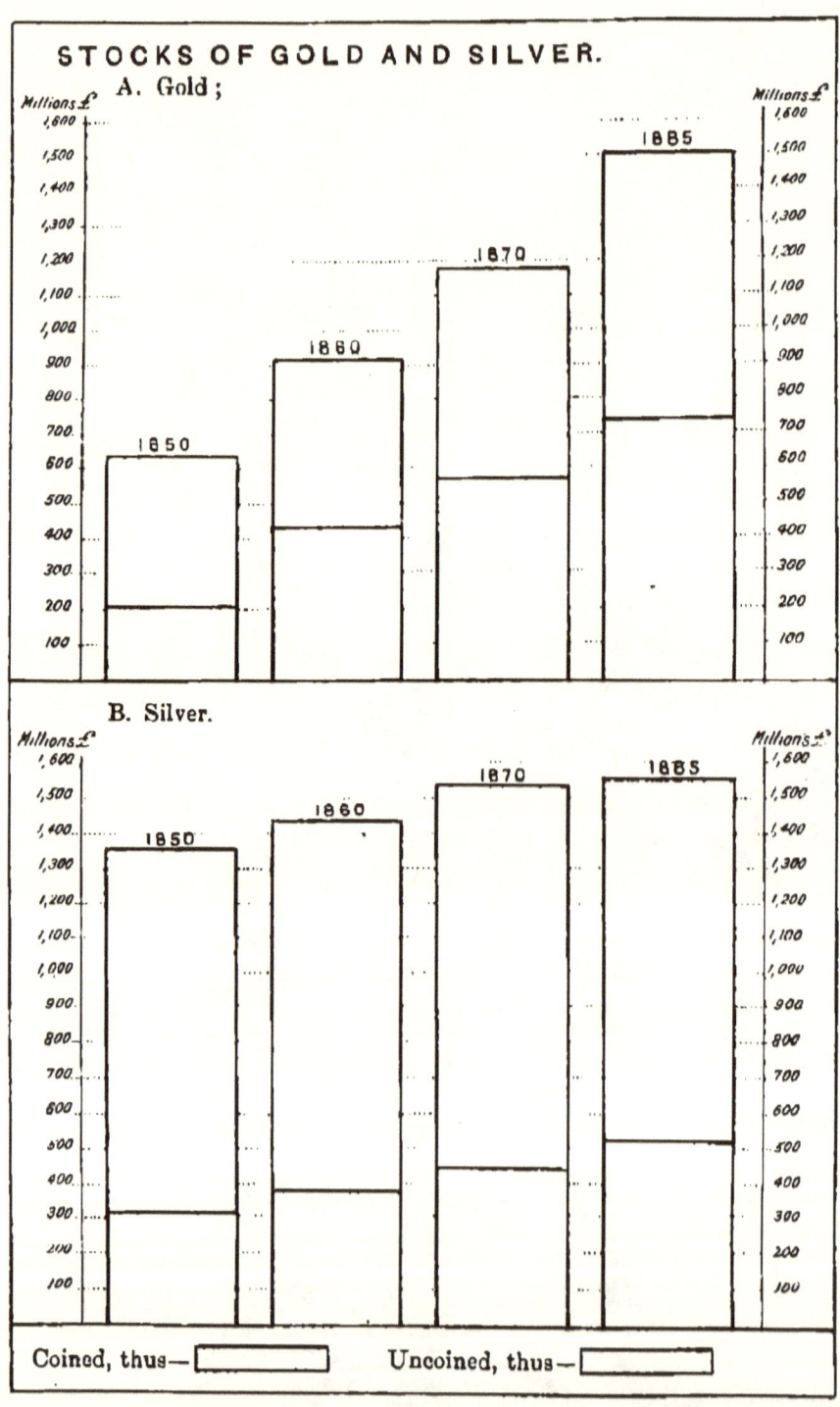

III.

THE PRECIOUS METALS.

So long as gold and silver are used in the purchase of commodities we must study their movement, although the best authorities (except Jevons) maintain that the supply of the precious metals has no perceptible effect on prices, a fact which the experience of the last thirty years fully confirms. In 1850, the world possessed a much smaller amount of gold and silver, coined and uncoined, than at present; the aggregate, measured in millions sterling, has risen 50 per cent., and prices, as we have seen, have fallen 5 per cent. The stock of the two metals is shown thus in millions £ :—

Year.	Gold.			Silver.			Grand Total.
	Coined.	Uncoined.	Total.	Coined.	Uncoined.	Total.	
1850	205	425	630	310	1,040	1,350	1,980
1860	433	478	911	370	1,060	1,430	2,341
1870	575	600	1,175	440	1,100	1,540	2,715
1885	736	768	1,504	520	1,030	1,550	3,054

The stock of gold is nearly two-and-a-half times what it was in 1850, while the quantity of silver has risen only 35 per cent., and the amount measured in value of this metal only 15 per cent. The decline of silver, which has fallen 20 per cent. since 1861, is not so much the result of over-production as of diminished use in manufacture, electro-plate having in great measure superseded it. The official returns of silver stamped in Great Britain for plate or ornament show an annual average of 1,091,000oz. in the years 1821-50, and only 790,000oz. in the decade ending 1880.

If we compare the actual tons weight of both metals at various dates we shall find that gold is relatively much more abundant than silver, judged by the ratio of previous years :—

	Tons, Coined and Uncoined.			Ratio.		
Year.	Gold.	Silver.	Total.	Gold.	Silver.	Total.
1850 .	4,550	148,000	152,550	3	97	100
1860 .	6,510	157,000	163,510	4	96	100
1870 .	8.390	169,000	177,390	5	95	100
1885 .	10,760	201,000	211,760	5	95	100

Thus the quantity of silver is now only nineteen times that of gold, whereas in 1850 it was thirty-two times, and yet, strange to say, silver has fallen.

If the price of the precious metals depended on the relative existing stocks, coined and uncoined, silver should at present be worth 102 pence per oz., or 70 per cent. more than in 1850. In other words, the actual quotation of silver (49 pence) would imply a stock of 410,000 tons, or more than double the reality. The truth is, as M'Culloch says, that no relation exists, and that "we should no more wonder to see silver falling when gold rises than if copper were to fall when lead rises." The value of silver compared with gold has been, since 1840, as follows :—

Year.	Pence per Oz.	Oz. to 1 Oz. Gold.	Year.	Pence per Oz.	Oz. to 1 Oz. Gold.
1840-50 .	60·5	15·6	1871-75 .	59·2	16·0
1851-55 .	61·5	15·3	1876 .	46·5	20·3
1856-60 .	61·5	15·3	1877-80 .	54·0	17·5
1861-65 .	61·2	15·4	1881-84 .	51·0	18·5
1866-70 .	60·5	15 6	1885 . .	49·0	19·3

The minimum was touched in 1876, when Prince Bismarck sold 3,200 tons of old German silver coin.

The production of gold since 1850 has been 6,260 tons, the loss from wear-and-tear, shipwreck, &c., close on 50 tons, leaving a net increase equal to 180 tons per annum.

It will be, meantime, more intelligible to state the production according to value, as follows :—

Millions £.

	1851-60.	1861-70.	1871-80.	1881-84.	Total.
United States	102	98	70	26	296
Australia	104	82	72	17	275
Russia	38	40	48	24	150
Other Countries	38	44	50	10	142
Total	282	264	240	77	863

Consumption during the whole period averaged 15 millions for coinage, and 10 millions for manufacture, but the coinage was greatest in the decade ending 1860. Expressed in value the consumption was as follows :—

Millions £.

Period.	Coinage.	Manufactures, &c.	Total.
1851-60	228	54	282
1861-70	142	122	264
1871-84	161	156	317
Total	531	332	863

Although the amount absorbed from the mines for coinage was 531 millions sterling, this by no means represents the value of gold coins minted in the said thirty-four years, which exceeded 1,080 millions ; the gold money of nations having been twice minted since 1850. More than 50 million napoleons, for example, were melted down for the new German gold currency.

As for silver, the production, in weight, has been as follows :—

Tons.

	1851-60.	1861-70.	1871-84.	Total.
Spanish America	5,500	7,100	13,800	26,400
United States	1,100	1,800	14,200	17,100
Germany, &c.	2,100	2,900	6,600	11,600
Total	8,700	11,800	34,600	55,100

Loss from wear-and-tear, shipwreck, &c., amounted to 4,000 tons, leaving a net increase of 51,000, that is 1,500, tons per annum. At present the loss of this metal is about 200 tons yearly, or one hundred times that of gold. Jevons shows that gold coin loses 2 per cent., silver 10 per cent., of their weight in 100 years.

Consumption of silver since 1850 has been as follows, in value :—

	Million £.		
Period.	Coinage.	Manufactures, &c.	Total.
1851-60	60	21	81
1861-70	70	40	110
1871-84	80	190	270
Total	210	251	461

Most of the coinage has been done in India, where the mint turned out in thirty-one years no less than 196 millions sterling. The United States began coining silver dollars in 1876, and the amount was increased by the Bland Law of 1878, since which time the average has been 6 million sterling per annum. In August 1885 the Washington Treasury had 32 million sterling of these dollars, and it is feared that Government may shortly have to pay the coupons of public debt in silver, entailing a loss of 18 or 20 per cent. on holders. It appears inevitable to repeal the Bland Act, and then silver will perhaps again go down to 46 pence, causing a further fall of 10 per cent. in Indian currency.

Notwithstanding the enormous increase of commerce, the quantity of precious metals sent over sea in exchange for commodities is less every year, at present barely exceeding 5 per cent. of the value of merchandise, against 12 per cent. in 1861-65. This may be ascribed partly to telegraphs, partly to the more extended use of cheques and bills of exchange. The amount of sea-borne treasure since 1861 has been :—

THE PRECIOUS METALS.

	Million £.			
Years.	Gold.	Silver.	Total.	Per annum.
1861–70	512	444	956	96
1871–83	647	493	1,140	88
Twenty-three years	1,159	937	2,096	91

Since 1880 the average has declined to 80 millions, or about 6 per cent. of the value of sea-borne merchandise, and it is still falling. The movement between the various countries, of coin and bullion, has been as follows, in millions sterling :—

	Gold.		Silver.		Total.	
	Imports.	Exports.	Imports.	Exports.	Imports.	Exports.
Great Britain	383	318	251	235	634	553
France	365	233	227	145	592	378
United States	104	196	36	106	140	302
Australia	21	203	...	...	21	203
India, &c.	286	209	423	451	709	660
Total	1,159	1,159	937	937	2,096	2,096

India and China absorbed 380 millions of silver, or 16½ millions per annum, say 42,000 tons in twenty-three years. In the same interval the world produced 44,000 tons, from which, deducting 3,000 for wear-and-tear, the net product was 41,000 tons. Thus it appears that India and China have taken since 1860 more than the total product of the mines, and if silver has become a drug, it is simply because its employment in manufacture is growing less, owing to the diminished use of silver plate.

The quantities of coin used in the different countries in 1850 and in 1884 were as follows, in millions sterling :—

	1850.			1884.		
	Gold.	Silver.	Total.	Gold.	Silver.	Total.
Great Britain	61	12	73	124	19	143
France	16	111	127	198	110	308
Germany	10	40	50	75	45	120
Russia	6	10	16	30	12	42
Austria	3	10	13	10	10	20
Italy	17	11	28	30	10	40
Spain and Portugal	15	15	30	38	17	55
Belgium and Holland	6	16	22	26	25	51
Scandinavia	2	2	4	5	2	7
Other countries	2	4	6	7	5	12
Europe	138	231	369	543	255	798
United States	34	6	40	130	50	180
India, &c.	4	55	59	63	215	278
Total	176	292	468	736	520	1,256

Gold money has increased 560 millions, silver 228, the aggregate being only half the amount of coin turned out by the various mints of the world in the said interval of thirty-four years, as we see from the official returns, viz.:—

Millions £ coined from 1850 to 1884.

	Gold.	Silver.	Total.
Great Britain	155	14	169
France	299	45	344
Germany	91	56	147
Russia	110	22	132
Other countries	96	118	214
Europe	751	255	1,006
United States	254	64	318
Australia	65	...	65
India	2	196	198
Total	1,072	515	1,587

Comparing the amount coined since 1850 with the actual increase of metallic money, we find that 48 per cent. of the gold and 55 per cent. of the silver have been simply re-minted, a fact overlooked by public speakers and writers when comparing the yield of the mines with the demand for coinage.

The quantity of coin necessary in any country depends on neither population nor trade. In Great Britain £4 per inhabitant is found enough, but in France they have £8. Two of the poorest countries in Europe, namely, Spain and Portugal, have the largest amount of metallic money compared to commerce, viz. :—

	Millions £.		
	Commerce.	Coin.	Coin Ratio.
Great Britain	700	143	20
France	360	308	85
Germany	350	120	34
Italy	102	40	40
Spain and Portugal	55	55	100
United States	310	180	58

The principal facts to be remembered touching the precious metals are:—

Firstly. That the world has now three and three-quarter times as much gold coin as in 1850.

Secondly. That only 48 per cent. of the gold above ground is used for coin.

Thirdly. That silver now forms only 41 per cent. of coined money, whereas it was 60 per cent. in 1850.

Fourthly. That the world now uses 70 per cent. more silver money than in 1850.

Fifthly. That the actual stock of silver is only nineteen times the weight of the stock of gold, whereas it was thirty-two times in 1850.

Sixthly. That if the metals were regulated in value by the existing stocks, the price of silver should now be 102 pence per oz., instead of 49 pence.

Seventhly. That since 1860 India and China have absorbed a little more than the total product of the silver-mines of the world.

Eighthly. That the fall in silver is because plate has gone out of fashion.

Ninthly. That sea-borne gold and silver are now less than 6 per cent. of the value of merchandise exchanged, against 12 per cent. in 1861–65.

Tenthly. That prices[1] are not regulated or even affected by the amount of metallic money per inhabitant, and that we make 20 shillings of coin in Great Britain do as much trade as 85 shillings in France, 40 in Italy, 58 in United States, or 100 in Spain.

---

[1] In no case in the present work do I take note of prices in inconvertible paper-money, which are really no prices until translated into gold equivalents.

IV.

THE MONEY MARKET.

ALTHOUGH prices do not move in sympathy with the rate of discount, it is evident that, directly or indirectly, the cost of production must be influenced by the value of money. Hence, if other conditions be equal, Great Britain has a considerable advantage over the rest of the world, because money is cheaper with us than elsewhere. The rate of interest, being the net profit on capital, has a downward tendency in countries where capital accumulates, and this tendency is manifested not only in England but generally all over Europe in the average rates of the last three decades, viz. :—

	Average Rates of Discount.			
	1851–60.	1861–70.	1871–80.	Fall since 1860.
Great Britain	4·17	4·23	3·28	0·89
France	4·30	3·55	3·94	0·36
Germany	4·05	4·56	4·30	...
Austria	5·26	4·77	4·79	0·47
Italy	5·35	5·69	4·85	0·50
Holland	3·60	3·98	3·40	0·20
Belgium	3·62	3·59	3·60	0·02
Continent	4·36	4·36	4·15	0·21
General average	4·27	4·30	3·71	0·56

The fall in Great Britain has been almost one-fourth, that is to say, the manufacturer or merchant can now borrow £4000 for the same amount payable in interest that £3000 would have taken before 1860; and as a merchant's or manufacturer's profits are usually at least double the market rate of interest, this fall is equivalent to a reduction of 2 per cent. in the cost of production.

Meantime the fall of interest on the European Continent has been less than ¼ per cent., equal to a saving of 5 per cent. in the price paid for the use of money; this lesser reduction may be either because the Great Powers have been so often at war as to alarm capital, or because the accumulations of wealth have been much less than in Great Britain. One thing is certain, that the rate of discount in England for 1871-80 was one-fourth less than for the Continent at large, and lower than the average of any country in Europe. The normal value of money in the United States is 8 per cent. Cheap money having such influence on manufacturing industry, the fall of interest is a strong element in our favour.

The returns of the Bank of England, which play so prominent a part in the money-market, may be summed up in averages since 1850 as follows:—

	Millions £.			Bank-rate per Cent.	Highest Year of		
	Issue.	Bullion.	Deposits.		Issue.	Deposits.	Rate.
1851–55	20·9	16·2	17·9	3·70	1853	1853	1854
1856–60	21·7	14·4	19·0	4·54	1856	1859	1857
1861–65	21·3	14·0	20·1	4·90	1865	1862	1864
1866–70	24·0	19·4	23·4	3·60	1868	1870	1866
1871–75	26·3	23·0	27·5	3·76	1875	1872	1873
1876–80	28·3	27·7	31·5	2·90	1879	1879	1878
1881–84	26·2	23·0	30·5	3·53	1881	1881	1882

The highest issue was in March 1879, namely, 31 millions, and the lowest in 1851, when it was but 19½ millions. The highest bullion reserve was in September 1879, amounting to 35½ millions, the lowest during the crisis of 1857, when it fell below 6½ millions. Deposits reached a maximum in June 1879, rising to 37¼ millions, the lowest year having been 1854, not reaching 15½ millions. The highest year of bank-rate was 1864, averaging 7½ per cent., the rate that year never exceeding 9 per cent.; it has twice reached 10 per cent., during the crises of 1857 and 1866. The lowest year was 1852 (average 2·22), the rate oscillating between 2 and 2½ per cent.

If we compare the issue and bullion-reserve of the great banks of Europe for ten years we find as follows :—

	Issue.			Bullion.			Bullion Ratio.	
	1875–77.	1878–82.	1883–84.	1875–77.	1878–82.	1883–84.	1875–77.	1883–84.
England	28	28	26	26	26	22	93	85
France	105	102	119	69	77	80	66	67
Germany	39	38	41	26	25	27	67	66
Austria	30	32	37	14	16	20	47	54
Belgium	13	13	14	5	4	4	40	30
Total	215	213	237	140	148	153	66	65

The returns of the London Clearing-House have recently shown a falling-off, but no allowance has been made for the altered purchasing power of gold. On the whole, we find a rapid growth of business, in spite of temporary retrogression. The actual returns of weekly transactions, and their equivalent in view of the higher value of gold, have been as follows :—

	Millions £ Weekly.	
Years.	Actual.	Equivalent to
1867–70	68	68
1871–80	100	112
1081–84	119	154

The average for the last four years was nominally 19 per cent. over the previous decade, but would have bought 37 per cent. more merchandise, which is the real measure of the increase of trade. It is necessary, therefore, to caution the public how they receive Sir John Lubbock's tables, which are numerically correct, but likely to lead many persons astray, as they are unaccompanied by comment or explanation.

Since 1850 the amount of new capital mobilised for loans

and railways has been from 250 to 300 millions per annum, viz. :—

Millions £ Sterling.

Period.	Loans.	Railways.	Total.	Ann. Average.
1851–70	2,386	1,636	4,022	201
1871–82	1,523	2,654	4,177	348
32 years	3,909	4,290	8,199	256

The countries which called up this large amount of capital have not always provided it, at least one-third, and possibly one-half, of the above total having been raised in England. The following table embraces from 1850 to the end of 1882 :—

Millions £ Sterling.

	Railways.	Loans.	Total.	Per Annum
Great Britain	545	140	685	21
France	444	730	1,174	37
Germany	387	190	577	18
Russia	290	460	750	23
Austria	242	294	536	17
Italy	102	486	588	18
Spain and Portugal	88	354	442	14
Other Countries	170	181	351	11
Europe	2,268	2,835	5,103	159
United States	1,292	540	1,832	57
British Colonies and India	284	260	544	17
Other Countries	446	274	720	23
Total	4,290	3,909	8,199	256

In some cases, such as Russia, there is a repetition, the State having expended some of the new loans on railways, but this will not seriously alter the amount of new capital mobilised. Moreover, in all the above countries numerous public companies have been created for mining, manufactures, telegraphs, gas, drainage, &c., which would swell the above amount to 10,000 millions, or something over 300 millions per annum.

The increase of banking is one of the most striking

features in the last thirty-five years, during which period this branch of business has absorbed 1800 millions, as we see by comparing the total amount of capital and deposits in banks with the amount in 1850, thus :—

	Millions £ in Banking.		
	1850.	1885.	Increase.
Great Britain	260	840	580
Continent	330	1,052	722
United States	212	530	318
Colonies	20	175	155
Total	822	2,597	1,775

The average of money used in banking to population is £24 per head in the United Kingdom, £6 in France or Germany, £4 on the Continent generally, £10 in United States, £11 in Canada, and £32 in Australia. So much has the taste for banking spread through all grades of society, that we find the working-classes have deposited 400 millions sterling in savings-banks since 1850, as we see from official returns of the various countries :—

	Millions £.			
	1850.	1860.	1870.	1884-85.
United Kingdom	30	41	53	90
France	3	14	27	74
Germany	5	16	35	110
Austria	19	28	40	88
Other Countries	11	28	50	91
Europe	68	127	205	453

The number of depositors and average amount of deposit for the whole of Europe at different dates were as follows :—

Year.	Millions £.	Depositors.	Average £.
1850	68	3,911,000	17·4
1860	127	6,695,000	19·0
1870	205	10,833,000	18·9
1885	453	20,780,000	21·7

So rapid an increase both in the amount of savings and in the number of depositors shows what an improvement has taken place in the condition of the working-classes.

Among causes that operate on the money-market we must not omit bankruptcy, which inflicts an annual loss on commerce, in some countries averaging 3 per cent., in others as much as 6 per cent., compared to the total value of import and export trade. The following table shows the average in recent years for three principal countries:—

	Bankruptcy, Millions £.			Dividend per Cent.	Loss Percentage to Commerce.
	Liabilities.	Assets.	Loss.		
Great Britain	31	10	21	32	3·0
France	10	2	8	20	2·2
United States	36	18	18	50	5·8
Total	77	30	47	39	3·5

Notwithstanding the oft-repeated complaints of depression, loss, bad trade, &c., we find that the number of failures is declining in Great Britain; whereas it has risen 60 per cent. in the United States in less than ten years, the annual averages having been as follows:—

	1875-80.	1881-84.
Great Britain	13,960	9,505
United States	6,290	8,880
Canada	805	954
Total	21,055	19,339

During the last seven years the average amount of liabilities to each failure was £2600 in Great Britain, £2700 in Canada, and £4200 in the United States.

British consols being closely connected with the money-market, it may be well to record the prices, thus:—

Years.	Average.	Highest.	Lowest.
1851-60	95	102 in 1852	85 in 1854
1861-70	92	96 ,, 1867	84 ,, 1866
1871-80	95	101 ,, 1880	91 ,, 1874
1881-83	101	103 ,, 1883	98 ,, 1881

The facts in this chapter that particularly bear on prices are—

First. That Great Britain may be said to have unlimited command of capital at a rate of interest one-fourth less than the Continent.

Secondly. That the average rate of interest in Europe is one-eighth less than twenty-five years ago, having fallen from $4\frac{1}{4}$ to $3\frac{3}{4}$ per cent.; that is to say, the use of £8,000 now costs no more than £7,000 in 1851-60.

Thirdly. That, as regards Great Britain, a merchant can now borrow £4,000 for the same interest as £3,000 would have cost before 1860.

Fourthly. That twenty years have elapsed since the bank rate was at 10 per cent., and hence that periodical crises have lost their regularity.

Fifthly. That bullion continues to accumulate in the great banks of Europe at the rate of 1 per cent. per annum.

Sixthly. That new capital is called up yearly averaging 300 millions, or about a million sterling each day.

Seventhly. That between fresh capital and deposits the business of banking absorbs 100 millions yearly, including 20 millions deposited in savings banks by the working-classes.

Eighthly. That loss by bankruptcy all over the world averages about $3\frac{1}{2}$ per cent. on the amount of commerce, and that United States bankrupts give the highest ratio of assets.

Ninthly. That the heavy fall of price-level since 1880 has not been disastrous in Great Britain, the average number of failures in 1881-84 being 32 per cent. less than in 1875-80.

V.

FINANCES.

PUBLIC expenditure has an indirect effect upon prices, for as the taxes are lighter, the inhabitants will have more money for the purchase of commodities, and this will cause the demand to be greater. Taxation is growing very rapidly in Europe, the revenues of 1884 being 86 per cent. over the average of twenty years preceding the Franco-German war, viz. :—

	Millions £.			Percentage Increase since 1869.
	1850-69.	1870-82.	1884.	
Great Britain	69	80	88	27
France	78	105	142	82
Germany	37	73	103	179
Russia	39	60	92	136
Austria	38	61	71	87
Italy	31	54	62	100
Spain and Portugal	27	36	42	55
Belgium and Holland	15	18	23	53
Scandinavia	6	9	9	50
Europe	340	496	632	86
United States	28	64	70	150
Australia	5	15	23	360
Canada	3	5	7	133
India	45	55	74	64
Total	421	635	806	92

Taxation has increased all round four times faster than population, partly because of expensive military armaments, partly by reason of the growth of public debts. At the same time labour has become more productive, the condition

FINANCES.

of the masses is improved, and the incidence of taxation (although now 40 shillings per head for the European average, against 28 shillings in 1860) is practically lighter than it was twenty-five years ago. The following table shows the expenditure compared to population:—

	Shillings per Inhabitant.			Ratio.		
	1850.	1860.	1884.	1850.	1860.	1884.
United Kingdom	40	50	50	100	125	125
France	35	46	74	100	132	211
Germany	17	18	44	100	106	258
Russia	13	15	20	100	115	154
Austria	26	28	39	100	108	150
Italy	31	38	41	100	123	131
Spain	20	27	41	100	135	205
United States	7	8	26	100	114	371
Canada	16	18	30	100	113	188
Australia	30	125	148	100	417	493

The total expenditure of sixteen principal nations from 1850 to 1884 has been:—

	Millions £.		
	Amount.	Per Annum.	Ratio.
Public administration	14,170	405	49·6
Military expenses	8,960	256	31·3
Interest on debt	5,460	156	19·1
Total	28,590	817	100·0

The amount of revenues received was 25,060 millions, the balance obtained by loans being 3,530 millions, or 101 millions per annum. But for the enormous increase of military expenditure the above deficit would not have exceeded 30 millions a year: the total maintenance of armies and navies cost 84 millions sterling in 1850 and 155 millions in 1884, an increase of 85 per cent., while the number of fighting men (on peace footing) increased only 35 per cent., viz.:—

	Millions £.		Fighting men, thousands.	
	1850.	1884.	1850.	1884.
Great Britain	15·4	28·9	187	249
France	18·7	32·1	394	580
Germany	11·7	23·2	352	466
Russia	15·8	30·5	657	870
Austria	10·1	12·3	287	301
Italy	4·5	12·2	146	290
Spain	3·0	6·8	101	150
Portugal	1·0	1·5	30	36
Belgium	1·0	1·8	40·	46
Holland	1·6	2·6	55	74
Denmark	0·5	0·9	27	37
Sweden and Norway	1·2	2·0	63	69
Europe	84·5	154·8	2,339	3,158

The average annual cost per combatant was £36 in 1850, and £49 in 1884; the ratio of combatants to population was 99 per 10,000 in the first-mentioned year, and has now risen to 101. Military expenditure in Europe was 7 shillings per inhabitant in 1850, whereas at present it exceeds 10 shillings, an increase of 42 per cent. The burthen entailed by the actual military establishments may be summed up thus: firstly, they take 4 per cent. of the able-bodied men of Europe from productive pursuits; secondly, they involve an expenditure of 155 millions sterling, equal to 3 per cent. of the gross earnings of all nations; thirdly, they withdraw from industry 400,000 horses, equal to a tax of 1 per cent. yearly on agriculture and trade. These three imposts make up 8 per cent. as the military burthen in Europe, against 1¼ per cent. in the United States. In the following table some countries are shown to suffer a much heavier burthen than the rest, and it is needless to say that they are "handicapped" in the race of industry.

FINANCES.

	Percentage of Military Burthens.			
	Blood.	Earnings.	Horses.	Total.
Great Britain	3·2	2·5	0·6	6·3
France	5·8	3·3	2·4	11·5
Germany	4·2	2·8	2·0	9·0
Russia	4·2	4·0	0·5	8·7
Austria	3·2	2·0	1·4	6·6
Italy	4·0	3·5	5·3	12·8
Spain and Portugal	3·3	3·0	2·6	8·9
Holland	7·4	3·0	1·5	11·9
Belgium	3·3	1·7	1·8	6·8
Denmark	7·4	2·1	0·6	10·1
Sweden and Norway	4·3	2·0	1·2	7·5
Europe	4·0	3·0	1·1	8·1
United States	0·3	0·9	0·1	1·3

Among European countries the burthen is lightest in Great Britain, being only half what it is in France or Italy. As the average for the Continent is 9 per cent., we may say that the cost of production of all commodities is enhanced 9 per cent. from St. Petersburg to the Mediterranean, and only 6¼ per cent. in Great Britain, another advantage in our manufacturing competition with foreign nations.

Public debt is only to be deplored when wasted by fraudulent or incompetent Ministers, or sunk in chimerical undertakings, or squandered in gunpowder, and even what is spent in wars is sometimes unavoidable. But the expenditure in India and our Colonies for railways, canals, harbours, drainage, and other productive works has been most beneficial, the colonists borrowing at 4 or 5 per cent., and increasing the public wealth in a far greater degree. Some European loans have likewise been for purposes of public utility. The following table shows the inversion of money raised by loans from 1850 to 1882 inclusive:—

War.	Millions £.	Peace.	Millions £.
Crimean	305	Railways and telegraphs	767
United States	474	Russian serfs	85
Franco-German	382	Roads and bridges	440
Russo-Turkish	211	City improvements	210
Ironclads, &c.	315	Sundries	314
	1,687		1,816

Thus it appears that rather more than half of the public debts so feelingly deplored by sentimental writers were caused by expenditure of the most beneficial kind.

Nothing can be more absurd than the method so common in newspapers and handbooks of measuring taxation and debt by the number of shillings per inhabitant; they should be compared with the earnings and capital of each country as follows:—

	Millions £.		Tax ratio.	Millions £.		Debt ratio.
	Earnings.	Taxes.		Wealth.	Debt.	
Great Britain	1,247	88	7·1	8,720	756	8·7
France	965	142	14·7	8,060	911	11·3
Germany	850	103	12·1	6,323	229	3·6
Russia	848	92	10·8	4,343	553	12·7
Austria	602	71	11·8	3,613	419	11·7
Italy	345	62	18·0	2,351	522	22·2
Spain	218	35	16·0	1,593	390	24·3
Belgium	120	13	10·8	806	62	7·7
Holland	104	10	9·6	987	80	8·1
Scandinavia	151	9	6·0	1,343	30	2·2
Europe	5,450	625	11·5	38,139	3,952	10·4
United States	1,420	70	4·9	9,495	305	3·2
Australia	133	23	17·3	590	120	20·3
Canada	118	7	6·0	650	40	6·1
Total	7,121	725	10·2	48,874	4,417	9·0

Interest on debt takes 180 millions yearly, or one-fourth of the total revenues: this does not include the service of local debts, as I have not included local taxes. The whole matter of local finances is outside the present field of inquiry; but I may mention that local taxes in 1882 summed up 224

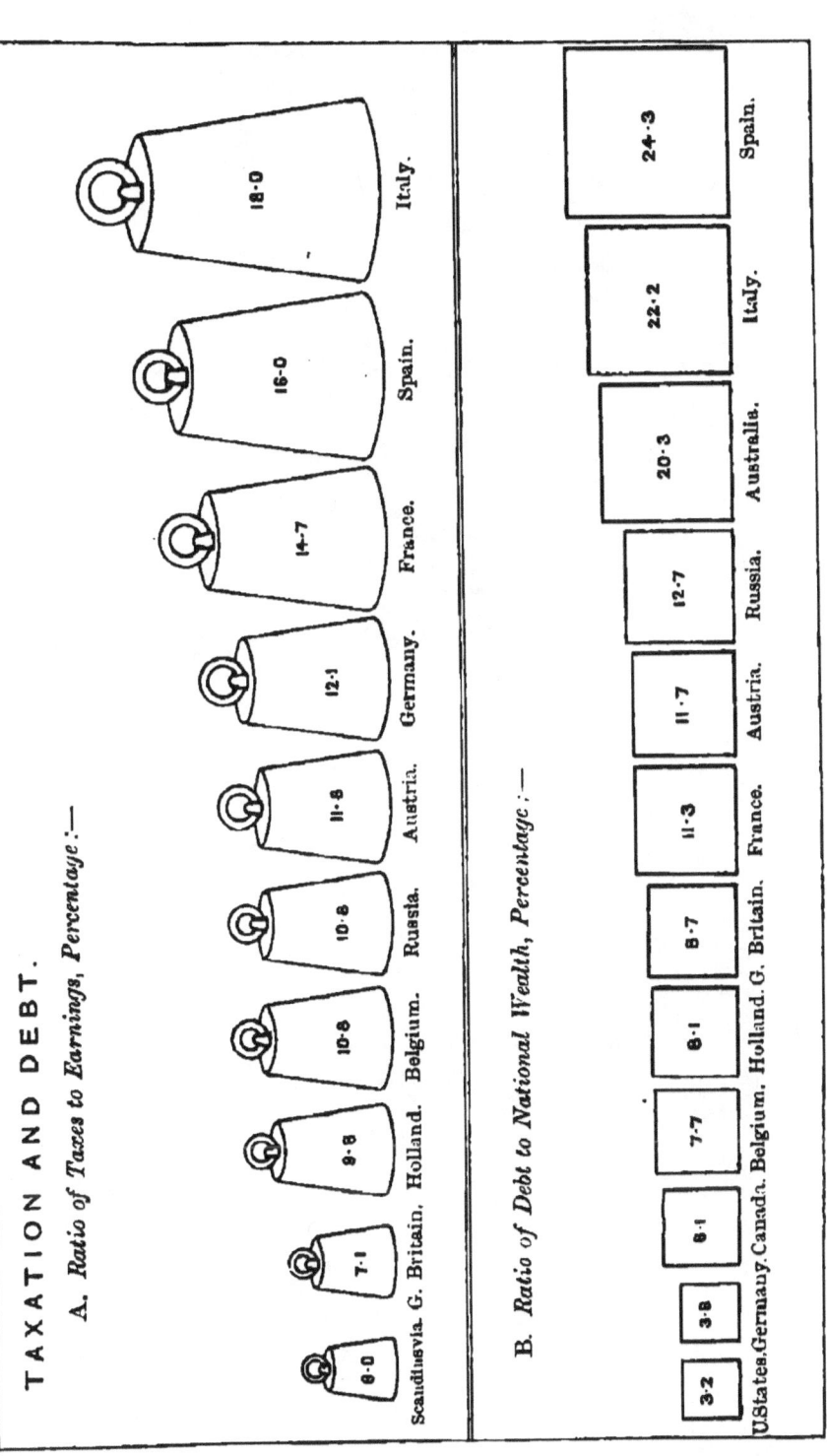

millions sterling, of which 84 millions in the United States, 38 millions in the United Kingdom, and the rest on the Continent. The local debt of Great Britain is already 160 millions, and continues rapidly in the ascendant.

The principal facts regarding finances that bear on prices are these:—

First. That as taxes have increased 92 per cent. in the last twenty years, or four times faster than population, this has tended to check the power of consumption among the masses throughout the world.

Secondly. That, at the same time, public wealth having grown in an unprecedented manner, the condition of the working-classes has so much improved that they now consume in all countries twice as much as in 1850, as shown by imports.

Thirdly. That military expenditure adds 9 per cent. on the Continent to cost of production, and in Great Britain only $6\frac{1}{4}$ per cent.

Fourthly. That the United Kingdom is, with one exception, the lightest taxed of European States.

Fifthly. That the average taxation of the world is $10\frac{1}{4}$ per cent. of earnings, and that Italy, Spain, and France so much exceed this ratio as to be considerably over-taxed.

Sixthly. That the public debt of the United Kingdom is $8\frac{3}{4}$ per cent. of capital, the general average for the Continent being 11 per cent.

Seventhly. That the Australian debt is exceptional, one-half of it being represented by State railways. Moreover, the unsold crown lands at 2 shillings per acre would suffice to redeem the whole debt.

Eighthly. That interest on public debts absorbs one-fourth of the public revenues of all nations.

Ninthly. That local taxes in the United States vastly exceed the general revenues of the republic.

Tenthly. That 52 per cent. of the debts of nations contracted since 1850 have been devoted to works of public utility, which effect a saving of 360 millions sterling yearly in cost of production and freight, equal to 7 per cent. on the sum of the world's products.

VI.

COMMERCE.

PRICES are so intimately connected with commerce, that we can hardly think of one without the other. It is the natural effect of commerce to bring prices as nearly as possible to a uniform level all over the world, and to this end railways and steam navigation have mainly co-operated. No longer do we see the inequalities of thirty years ago, when the value of the same commodity was often 50 per cent. higher in one place than in another only a hundred miles distant. The tendency of commerce on the whole is to a lower level of prices, since it stimulates production, and, as Professor Sidgwick observes—"It is a well-known law of industry that with every increase of the quantity produced the relative cost of production is diminished."

The amount of imports and exports of all nations, measured by value, has increased since 1850 no less than 283 per cent., or ten times faster than population, as appears from the following table :—

	Millions Sterling.					Per inhab. in 1884. £
	1850.	1860.	1870.	1880.	1884.	
Great Britain	193	376	547	698	686	19·0
France	75	167	227	339	315	8·4
Germany	105	160	212	315	331	7·0
Russia	32	46	100	121	114	1·3
Austria	29	51	83	128	137	3·5
Italy	26	46	74	96	99	3·4
Spain and Portugal	20	30	41	64	74	3·5
Holland	44	56	71	121	144	34·2
Belgium	35	48	64	116	116	20·3
Scandinavia	17	30	42	55	66	7·4
Europe	576	1,010	1,461	2,053	2,082	7·0
United States	64	137	172	309	276	4·9
South America	38	62	85	101	104	3·9
India and Colonies	93	192	241	362	451	2·3
The World	771	1,401	1,959	2,825	2,913	5·0

The volume of trade has increased much more than would appear from the foregoing table, for if prices had remained unchanged since 1850, the amounts would have been very different. The following table shows the growth of trade in thirty-four years, both as measured by value and by volume, viz. :—

Year.	Millions Sterling.		Development.		Price-Level.
	Actual Amount.	Price of 1850.	In Value.	In Volume.	
1850	771	771	100	100	100
1860	1,401	1,247	182	162	112
1870	1,959	1,783	254	232	110
1880	2,825	2,853	367	370	99
1884	2,953	3,278	383	426	90

If, therefore, no change of prices had occurred, the trade of last year would have represented four and a quarter times the amount in 1850, that is, an increase of 326 per cent., or twelve times greater than the progress of population. But if we come to consider the actual weight of merchandise carried between nations, we find that it has risen to six times the volume of 1850, owing to the fact that reduced freights have

OCEAN CARRYING TRADE.

A. *Tons of Merchandise Carried by all flags.*

B. *Tons of Merchandise Carried on British Bottom.*

Note.—Although steamers are used in the diagram, the figures express all cargo carried by steam or sail.

COMMERCE.

permitted an extraordinary development in articles of bulk and minor value. The following table shows the weight and value of merchandise exchanged at various dates:—

Year.	Weight Carried. Million Tons.	Value. Million £.	Value. £ per Ton.	Development.	
				Tonnage.	Value.
1850	25·1	347	13·9	100	100
1860	40·2	636	15·9	160	182
1870	69·0	882	12·8	275	254
1880	123·0	1,270	10·3	490	367
1884	152·0	1,330	8·8	602	383

If the character of the merchandise were the same, we should have evidence here that the price-level of the world had fallen 37 per cent. since 1850, whereas the actual fall has been only 10 per cent., as shown above. Coming later down, and comparing present returns with those for 1860, we find that in twenty-four years the carrying trade has quadrupled, while the value of merchandise carried has only doubled, the average value of a ton of goods having fallen 45 per cent. This is partly explained by the great increase in articles of bulk, viz. :—

	Sea-borne Merchandise. Tons, 000's omitted.				Ratio.	
	1860.	1861–70.	1871–80.	1883.	1860.	1883.
Coal	7,850	14,300	22,400	42,600	100	542
Iron	1,070	1,880	3,610	9,400	100	874
Grain	3,933	4,410	10,100	16,200	100	920
Sugar	960	1,190	1,960	2,910	100	415
Cotton	570	490	992	1,580	100	277
Meat	100	120	380	920	100	445
Wool	101	120	252	450	100	303
Sundries	25,629	32,490	56,306	78,440	100	310
Total	40,204	55,000	96,000	152,500	100	380

The quantity of coal carried over sea in 1883 was greater than the total weight of merchandise in 1860, and that of grain would have fed for twelve months a population of 102 million souls. It is very short-sighted for some people to assert that shipping should not increase faster than the value of commerce, for we see that the number of tons to be carried has quadrupled since 1860, and if shipping had only doubled its carrying power (that is, increased on a par with the value of trade), one-half of the world's merchandise would have been left without means of transport. Articles of bulk would not pay the cost of freight if shipping did not multiply twice as fast as the nominal amount of trade.

The balance of trade in Europe for twenty years ending 1880 showed an annual average of 157 millions sterling of imports over exports, that is, 22 per cent.; the sum-total for all nations averaged 128 millions excess of imports, or $12\frac{1}{2}$ per cent., which represented the cost of freight, insurance, and merchant's charges. The annual average for twenty years, 1861-80, was as follows:—

	Millions £.			Millions £.	
	Imports.	Exports.		Imports.	Exports.
Great Britain	321	245	Europe	869	712
France	132	125	United States	74	74
Germany	134	98	Canada	17	14
Russia	38	38	Australia	35	27
Austria	44	43	India	33	56
Italy	42	35	China and Japan	27	25
Spain and Portugal	24	20	South America	56	59
Belgium	43	34	Egypt	6	16
Holland	47	34	Java	7	13
Scandinavia	26	21	Various	27	27
Greece, &c.	18	19	The World	1,151	1,023

The average weight of merchandise over the whole period of twenty years was $75\frac{1}{2}$ million tons per annum; and if we compare with it the difference between imports and exports, it appears that each ton of merchandise paid 34 shillings between freight, insurance, and merchant's charges.

As whatever tends to impede trade is inimical to the interests of mankind, we must deplore the revival of protective tariffs, which, as Nassau Senior said of the balance-of-trade theories, " have caused more misery and misfortune than all the errors that ignorance has entailed on nations." The Governments of the European Continent collect in import dues 30 millions sterling more than they did twenty years ago, as appears from official returns, viz. :—

	Import Dues, Annual Average. Millions Sterling		Average " Ad Valorem," per cent.	
	1866-67.	1881-83.	1866-67.	1881-83.
France	4·0	13·2	4	7
Germany	4·1	10·2	4	7
Russia	4·2	9·0	12	11
Austria	2·0	3·4	8	5
Italy	2·4	5·6	7	11
Spain and Portugal	3·6	6·1	22	16
Holland, &c.	2·7	5·2	3	4
Continent	23·0	52·7	6	7
United States	35·5	43·0	40	31
Canada	1·2	4·4	7	18
Australia	3·4	6·3	11	11
India	2·4	4·2	8	8
Brazil	3·3	7·1	22	40
Argentine	1·5	3·6	24	28
Chili	0·7	2·4	14	22
Foreign countries	71·0	123·7	8	8

In the same period the import dues of Great Britain have been reduced 2½ millions sterling, the average for 1881-83 being 19½ millions sterling, which is less than 5 per cent. (4·7) of the value of imports, against 7 per cent. in 1866-67. The ratio of import dues in Europe (Continent) is now 45 pence per inhabitant, against 22 pence in 1866-67; that is, they have more than doubled. In the common interests of humanity it is desirable that all nations should hold a convention, like the Geneva Postal Treaty, to stipulate that no country shall impose duties which in the aggregate will exceed 10 per cent. of the value of imported merchandise. Higher duties are barbarous.

The effects of high and low tariffs are visible in the coutrast between Great Britain and the United States since 1841, viz. :—

	Import Dues Compared to Imports.		Total Commerce. Annual Average per Inhabitant.	
Period.	Gt. Britain, per cent.	U. States, per cent.	Gt. Britain. £	U. States. £
1841–50	27	23	5·8	2·2
1851–60	16	20	9·8	3·7
1861–70	8	36	16·1	2·4
1871–84	5	32	19·0	4·9

The British tariff has been reduced four-fifths, while that of the United States is now relatively 40 per cent. more than in 1841–50. As a natural result the trade *per inhabitant* of the United Kingdom has risen 228 per cent. against 123 per cent. in the United States. There would have been a still greater development of British trade if our colonies had not imposed duties on British manufactures, which so far paralysed or rather diminished their commerce with the mother country, that they now transact 58 per cent. of their trade with foreigners, and only 42 per cent. with the United Kingdom. Nevertheless, our commerce with the Colonies and India is growing faster than with other nations, viz. :—

	British Trade, Imports and Exports Together.					
	Millions Sterling			Percentage.		
With	1855.	1870.	1883.	1855.	1870.	1883.
Colonies	62	120	189	23·8	21·9	25·9
United States	44	81	136	16·9	14·8	18·6
Other countries	154	347	407	59·3	63·3	55·5
Total	260	548	732	100·0	100·0	100·0

Great Britain is increasing her relations with the people of her own kindred in the United States and the Colonies in preference to dealing with foreigners. Between Great Britain, the United States, and Colonies, the Anglo-Saxon race stands for half the trade of the world, the percentages being as follows :—

Commerce of the World.

	1850.	1860.	1870.	1880.	1884.
Great Britain	25·1	26·8	27·9	24·3	24·6
Colonies	12·0	13·7	12·3	12·9	15·3
British Empire	37·1	40·5	40·2	37·2	39·9
United States	8·3	9·8	8·7	10·9	9·3
France	9·7	12·0	11·5	12·0	10·7
Germany	13·6	11·4	10·8	11·1	11·2
Other countries	31·3	26·3	28·8	28·8	28·9
	100·0	100·0	100·0	100·0	100·0

It is a striking commentary on the fiscal system of the United States, that although their population has doubled in the last twenty-five years, they hold a smaller share of the trade of the world than in 1860. No country except Great Britain exceeds (or even approaches) the aggregate trade of the British Colonies.

The principal points in this chapter are :—

First. That the nominal amount of commerce has doubled since 1860, while the weight of merchandise has quadrupled, the average value of a ton of goods having fallen 45 per cent.

Secondly. That this is mainly due to the great increase in articles of bulk, such as coal, iron, grain, &c., some of which have grown ninefold.

Thirdly. That the balance of trade in twenty years averaged 22 per cent. imports more than exports for Europe, and 33 per cent. for Great Britain.

Fourthly. That the returns show an almost even balance of trade in poor countries, like Spain and Russia, and a large excess of imports in rich ones.

Fifthly. That all merchandise when converted from exports into imports acquires an additional value of 12½ per cent., covering freight, insurance, and charges, and that this averaged 34 shillings a ton in twenty years ending 1880.

Sixthly. That all import duties over 10 per cent. are, as a

rule, barbarous; and that the aggregate of duties should never exceed 10 per cent. of the value of imports in any civilised country.

Seventhly. That when some nations, such as Brazil, United States, Argentine Republic, and Chili, levy duties collectively exceeding 20 per cent., and in some of these countries reaching 40 per cent. of the total value of import trade, an artificial high level of prices is created most injurious to such countries.

VII.

SHIPPING.

FREIGHT enters so largely into the cost of commodities, averaging 10 per cent. on the value of sea-borne merchandise, that shipping has a direct influence on prices. We have just seen (page 36) that in twenty years ending 1880 each ton of goods paid 34 shillings between the port of shipment and that of destination, 80 per cent. of this sum being for freight, say 27 shillings; but in 1884 the difference of value between imports and exports was only 23 shillings, the freight therefore not exceeding 18 shillings per ton. Thus it appears that freights all over the world have declined 33 per cent., and that consequently merchandise can be sold at a reduction of 9 shillings per ton, or 5 per cent., as compared with the mean average of 1861–80. The price-level for 1884 being 15 per cent. lower than the mean level of the said twenty years, we find that one-third of the so-called depression of trade is simply an economy of freight.

Although the weight of merchandise carried by sea has multiplied sixfold since 1850, the tonnage of merchant shipping has only trebled, as shown in the subjoined table :—

Year.	Tons Shipping, 000's omitted.	Merchandise. Million Tons.	Tons Carried. Per Ton Shipping.
1850	6,905	25·1	3·6
1860	10,406	40·2	3·9
1870	15,576	69·0	4·4
1883	21,640	152·0	7·1

Seeing that 100 tons of shipping now carry twice as much merchandise as in 1850, there is an apparent saving of 50 per cent. in wages and all other sea-going expenses. The greater efficiency of shipping is mainly the result of steam navigation, no less than 72 per cent. of the world's merchandise having been carried by steamers in 1884. The following table shows the rapid increase of steamers :—

Omitted 000's.

Year.	Shipping, Nominal Tonnage.		Tons Carried by		Steam Ratio in	
	Steamers.	Sailing Vessels.	Steamers.	Sailing.	Nominal Tonnage, per cent.	Carrying Power, per cent.
1850	392	6,513	5,850	19,230	5½	23
1860	820	9,586	12,040	28,120	8	30
1870	1,918	13,868	28,020	41,100	12½	41
1883	7,330	14,310	109,450	42,630	34	72

In 1883 steamers made fifteen, sailing vessels three, trips during the year, as we find by comparing their tonnage with the port-entries of nations—hence a steamer has five times the carrying power of a sailing vessel of same tonnage. Shipowners usually consider the difference as three to one, which is true of long voyages; but in short ones a steamer makes eight, while a sailing vessel would make one; as, for example, from Dublin to Liverpool, or from Hull to Hamburg.

The economy of labour resulting from steam navigation and other changes in shipping is shown in the average of tons of merchandise borne by British seamen, viz. :—

Year.	Seamen.	Million Tons Carried.	Tons per Seaman.
1850	148,000	15	101
1860	172,000	23	135
1870	196,000	36	184
1883	201,000	78	388

It has been already shown (p. 39) that the commerce of the British Empire is 40 per cent. of that of the world, but our portion of the carrying trade is much greater, namely, 58 per cent., that is, 51 per cent. by the shipping of the

SHIPPING.

United Kingdom and 7 per cent. by Colonial vessels. The following table shows the tonnage and carrying trade of the various flags in 1883 :—

Flag.	Nominal Tonnage. (Omitted 000's.)			Tons Carried.	Tons Carried per		Ratio of Carrying Trade.
	Steam.	Sailing.	Total.		Seamen.	Ship.	
British	3,728	3,514	7,242	78,100	388	4,110	51·1
Colonial	201	1,953	2,154	10,540	176	1,520	6·9
British Empire	3,929	5,467	9,396	88,640	340	3,430	58·0
United States	1,403	2,832	4,235	6,940	308	2,700	4·5
France	467	536	1,003	10,250	294	3,330	6·7
Germany	375	895	1,270	9,890	250	3,010	6·5
Italy	107	866	973	5,010	102	1,640	3·3
Spain	164	374	538	4,260	196	2,340	2·8
Norway and Sweden	170	1,890	2,060	9,780	128	1,560	6·5
Other flags	715	1,450	2,165	17,730	185	2,220	11·7
Total	7,330	14,310	21,640	152,500	252	2,750	100·0

Our supremacy on sea has been erroneously ascribed to "the facility with which we can build iron vessels," as if the builders on the Tyne or the Clyde would not as readily construct a steamer for a Frenchman or an American as for an Englishman ! The secret lies partly in the superior efficiency of our shipping, partly in the protective laws of the United States, France, and some other countries, which put penalties on vessels not built at home, thus indirectly helping to transfer to us a still larger portion than before of the carrying trade of the seas. The superior efficiency of our shipping, as shown in the preceding table, is very remarkable, each seaman aboard British vessels carrying 388 tons, that is, as much as two Spanish or four Italian sailors. Not that the Englishman is more dexterous than the Italian (who is an excellent seaman), but because our pre-eminence in steamers makes a great difference, and also the size of our vessels, large ones being more economical of hands. During the last fifteen years the average tonnage of ships has risen

50 per cent., the Suez Canal returns showing that on that route it has risen from 905 tons in 1870 to 2,150 in 1881–83. In the foregoing table it may seem strange that the United States shipping represents so little carrying trade as 7 million tons, but this is because most of their vessels are mainly occupied in the lakes and other internal waters, of which the business is not here included, the table referring only to the high seas.

The decline of American shipping in ocean traffic since 1860 is shown by the diminished ratio of United States trade carried in American bottom, viz. :—

Year.	United States Imports and Exports, Million £.		Ratio.	
	American Flag.	Foreign Flags.	American.	Foreign.
1860	106	53	67	33
1870	67	123	35	65
1880	58	273	17	83
1882	51	269	16	84

The relative decline of French shipping is no less remarkable, in spite of the differential duties levied on British and other foreign vessels. The port-entries in France averaged as follows :—

Period.	Tons, 000's omitted.		Percentage.	
	French Flag.	Other Flags.	French.	Other.
1860–64	1,910	2,850	40	60
1872–76	2,605	5,417	33	67
1880–83	3,908	8,912	30	70

The shipping-bounties decreed by the French Chambers in 1880 consist of a bonus of 48 shillings per ton for building vessels in French workshops, and £6 per 100 tons for every 1000 miles run by French vessels : these bounties average £400,000 per annum, and yet the ratio of French shipping declines.

In Italy the ratio of foreign (chiefly British) shipping is likewise increasing : it was 65 per cent. in 1872–76, and 70 per cent. in 1880–83.

SHIPPING. 45

In Germany there has been no change, the foreign (mostly British) ratio being still 60 per cent., the same as ten years ago.

In Spain, notwithstanding an oppressive customs system, the ratio of foreign (mostly British) shipping rose to 72 per cent. in 1880–82, against 65 per cent. in 1872–76.

So great has been the increase of trade in the last ten or fifteen years, that other nations have been unable to build vessels fast enough, and but for British shipping, no country in the world (except Canada, Sweden, and Norway) would have sufficient vessels to carry on its commerce. From time to time we hear a wail of distressed British ship-owners, as if a great portion of our merchant navy were laid up, whereas the shipping of the United Kingdom (without Colonial) carried in 1883 no less than 51 per cent. of the world's commerce, a proof that our vessels and seamen are not idle. Nor is there an increase in ballast entries of the United Kingdom, the ratio having declined since 1875 from 21 to 18 per cent. of total entries.

The value of merchandise imported by five countries of Europe compared with the tonnage of entries gives the following averages:—

	£ per Ton.			Ratio.	
	1860.	1870.	1883.	1860.	1883.
Great Britain	17·6	16·5	13·3	100	76
France	25·1	20·6	17·1	100	68
Italy	15·3	10·6	9·6	100	64
Holland	27·0	28·3	21·7	100	80
Belgium	29·0	23·5	26·1	100	90
Medium	22·8	19·9	17·6	100	77

The chief points in this chapter are these:—

First. That shipping earned 27s. per ton on all sea-borne merchandise in 1861–80, and only 18s. in 1884, thus reducing the cost of all commodities by 9s. per ton, or 5 per cent. of the value.

Secondly. That the reduction of freight is due to greater efficiency of shipping, one British seaman now carrying as much as two in 1870, three in 1860, or four in 1850.

Thirdly. That this greater efficiency is mainly the result of steam navigation, and that steamers now carry 72 per cent. of the world's merchandise, or nearly twice the ratio of 1870.

Fourthly. That steamers have five times the carrying power of sailing vessels of equal tonnage.

Fifthly. That British vessels carry 51 per cent. of all seaborne merchandise, one British seaman carrying as much as two Spanish or four Italian.

Sixthly. That the medium value of a ton of imported merchandise in Europe was £23 in 1860, falling to £20 in 1870, and to £17$\frac{1}{2}$ in 1883.

Seventhly. That the shipping-bounties, which cost France £400,000 per annum, are unable to check the *relative* decline of French shipping.

Eighthly. That British shipping is every year increasing in the ratio of port-entries in France, Italy, Spain, United States, and several other countries.

Ninthly. That ballast-entries are not increasing in ratio in the United Kingdom, but have declined since 1875.

Tenthly. That but for the activity of British shipbuilders in the past ten years, the commerce of all nations would have been paralysed, or at least seriously diminished, for want of vessels.

VIII.

RAILWAYS AND TELEGRAPHS.

RAILWAYS hold on land the same position as shipping on sea, and have exercised the most powerful of all influences on prices: they may be said to date from 1850, in which year the total length of existing lines did not reach 25,000 miles, or one-twelfth of the actual mileage. The following table shows their development down to 1883, the latest year for which we have complete returns:—

	Miles.				
	1850.	1860.	1870.	1880.	1883.
United Kingdom	6,621	10,433	15,537	17,945	18,668
France	1,882	5,903	11,106	16,213	18,023
Germany	3,664	7,056	11,805	21,317	22,549
Russia	310	994	7,046	14,802	16,617
Austria	940	2,802	5,915	11,543	12,321
Italy	380	1,373	3,865	5,492	5,803
Spain	202	1,204	3,256	4,661	5,555
Portugal	...	89	445	778	1,039
Switzerland	196	660	890	1,652	1,735
Roumania	...	...	153	870	922
Turkey	...	40	180	1,042	1,062
Belgium	560	1,080	1,812	2,570	2,634
Holland	110	205	890	1,122	1,263
Denmark	20	70	470	990	1,105
Sweden and Norway	...	420	1,322	4,373	4,900
Europe	14,885	32,329	64,692	105,370	114,196
United States	9,072	30,810	53,224	94,225	121,180
Canada	410	1,890	2,695	6,932	9,066
Spanish America	120	850	2,940	8,390	13,558
Australia	...	360	1,040	4,890	6,103
India	...	850	4,802	9,215	10,832
Java	...	...	90	280	442
Egypt	...	290	660	927	942
Algeria	...	...	170	880	1,095
South Africa	...	...	70	1,020	1,650
Other countries	...	...	290	608	996
The World	24,487	67,379	130,673	232,737	280,060

Thirty years ago the ordinary cost of land-carriage for goods, in Europe, was £3 a ton per 100 miles, or six times what it is at present. Thus we have here a saving of 50s. a ton; and as the medium value of merchandise in 1850 (see page 35) was £14 per ton, the saving caused by railways has been equal to 9 per cent. on the wholesale price.

The amount of labour and capital expended by the present generation, that is, in a period of thirty-five years, in the construction of railways, is prodigious, the cost of existing lines being over 5,000 millions sterling, a sum exactly equal to the nominal amount of the public debt of the world; so that the present generation may be said to balance its accounts with the next by handing over to it a species of newly-created property which covers all the State debts that are so often and so feelingly alluded to by shallow sentimentalists as a mortgage on the industry of posterity. The capital expended on railways at various dates has been as follows:—

	Millions Sterling.			
	1850.	1860.	1870.	1883.
Great Britain	240	348	530	785
Continent	134	356	890	2,017
United States	60	225	480	1,352
Colonies, &c.	7	50	177	577
The World	441	979	2,077	4,731

From 1870 until 1880 the annual average of new capital put into railways was almost 200 millions, and since 1881 it has risen to 300 millions, that is, about 1 million sterling daily, equal to 60 miles of new line, with rolling-stock. If we call to mind that the annual savings of Great Britain, the European Continent, and the United States, average 644 millions (see page 288 of "Dictionary of Statistics") in the aggregate, it will appear that one-half of the savings of mankind is yearly absorbed in new railways.

RAILWAYS AND TELEGRAPHS.

Goods traffic has increased since 1850 much faster by railway than by shipping, as appears in the following table:—

	Millions of Tons Carried.			Ratio.	
Year.	By Rail.	By Shipping.	Total.	Rail.	Shipping.
1850	97	25	122	80	20
1860	193	40	233	83	17
1870	602	69	671	90	10
1883	1,080	152	1,232	88	12

The goods traffic of the world sums up 4 million tons daily, or ten times what it was in 1850, and employs about 2 million men, who move on an average 2 tons each for a distance of 100 miles. The ordinary freight-charge by railway in various countries is as follows:—

Pence per Ton, per 100 Miles.

United States	63	Holland	118
Belgium	70	Great Britain	135
Germany	84	France	154
Italy	108	Sweden	160
Austria	111	Average	111

If other things be equal, the difference of railway freight must cause a difference of prices between countries: Belgium, for example, pays only half what is charged in Great Britain, and a difference of 65 pence per ton is equal to about 2 per cent. of the ordinary value of merchandise. Moreover, the passenger fares indirectly affect prices, for it is plain that if they could be simultaneously reduced all over Europe the cost of distribution would be so far lessened as to cause a fall of prices. They are much higher in this country than on the Continent, viz.:—

	Pence per 100 Miles.				Pence per 100 Miles.		
	1st Cl.	2d Cl.	3d Cl.		1st Cl.	2d Cl.	3d Cl.
Belgium	115	85	56	Austria	180	135	90
Scandinavia	155	105	68	Russia	182	136	77
Germany	155	115	77	France	192	144	105
Holland	160	135	77	Spain	200	154	95
Italy	173	125	85	Great Britain	230	160	95

The excuse offered for such high tariffs in Great Britain is that the cost of construction has been double the European average, and it appears also that the numerous Boards of Directors add considerably to working expenses.

The traffic returns of the United Kingdom show the following results :—

£ Per Mile.

	1860.	1870.	1880.	1884.
Earnings	2,670	2,810	3,659	3,740
Expenses	1,270	1,402	1,877	1,970
Profits	1,400	1,408	1,782	1.770

The net result for capital in 1883 was 4·4 in England, 3·7 in Scotland, 3·6 in Ireland, and 4·3 for the United Kingdom.

Telegraphs have exercised a lesser, but unquestionable, effect towards the fall in prices, by enabling merchants to work with less capital, to keep smaller stocks of commodities, and to turn over their money oftener. The following table shows the mileage and number of messages for the principal countries in 1883 :—

	Miles.	Million Messages.	Messages per 100 Inhabitants.
United Kingdom	27,100	32·8	90
France	47,900	19·5	52
Germany	46,400	18·4	40
Russia	69,400	9·8	11
Austria	30,860	9·8	25
Italy	17,250	6·5	22
Spain and Portugal	13,300	5·1	25
Holland and Belgium	5,830	10·2	90
Scandinavia	16,400	3·2	36
Switzerland	4,300	3·0	108
United States	154,650	65·0	120
Canada	11,000	1·4	30
Spanish America	47,700	4·1	11
Australia	30,700	5·6	180
Cape Colony	9,600	0·7	60
India	22,600	2·1	1

The above does not include 110,000 miles of ocean-cables, which with the land-lines make up a total of exactly 700,000 miles; the number of messages in 1883 was 210 millions, and at present averages 20 millions monthly.

The points in this chapter which bear on prices are these :—

First. That railways have reduced land-carriage to one-sixth of the previous charges, and thus saved 50 shillings per ton.

Secondly. That this saving is equal to a reduction of 9 per cent. in the value or price of commodities in general.

Thirdly. That railway freights in Great Britain are 17 per cent. over the average on the Continent, and more than double those of United States.

Fourthly. That the difference of goods freight between the Continent and Great Britain is such, that if the Continental average ruled here we could produce and sell merchandise nearly 1 per cent. cheaper than at present.

Fifthly. That British industry is handicapped by excessive railway tariffs both for goods and passengers.

Sixthly. That the goods traffic of the world sums up 4 million tons daily, carried for an average distance of 100 miles, at a cost of 8 shillings, and employing two million men. The same traffic in 1850 was under 400,000 tons daily.

Seventhly. That telegraphs have helped to lower cost of production and prices, but how far cannot be ascertained.

IX.

STEAM-POWER.

UNDER a variety of forms steam-power reduces the cost both of production and distribution to such a degree that we can hardly measure its effect on prices, the steam horse-power of the world being now six times what it was in 1850, viz. :—

Year.	Horse-power of Engines, 000's omitted.			
	Fixed.	Railway.	Steamboat.	Total.
1850	1,785	4,190	340	6,315
1860	2,450	7,900	1,050	11,400
1870	3,650	13,700	2,190	19,540
1880	7,415	17,618	3,891	28,930
1885	10,500	19,400	5,200	35,100

In recent years the increase has averaged one million horse-power per annum, and the distribution among nations is shown as follows :—

	Horse-power, 000's omitted.				
	1850.	1860.	1870.	1880.	1885.
United Kingdom	2,320	3,100	4,780	7,786	9,740
Continent	1,990	4,220	8,980	12,992	14,820
United States	2,005	4,080	5,780	8,152	10,540
Total	6,315	11,400	19,540	28,930	35,100

This total of 35 million horse-power is used to drive 71,000 locomotives, 9200 steamboats, and 430,000 fixed engines. As steam can work by day and night, requiring no rest for sleep or food, its actual power is three times greater than if the work were done by horses. The distribution in 1885 is as follows:—

	Horse-power, 000's omitted.			
	Fixed.	Railway.	Steamboat.	Total.
United Kingdom	3,100	3,500	3,140	9,740
Continent	4,100	9,700	1,020	14,820
United States	3,300	6,200	1,040	10,540
Total	10,500	19,400	5,200	35,100

Summing up the work that is accomplished daily among all nations by hand, by horses, and by steam-power, between agriculture, mining, manufactures, transport, &c.—that is, allowing 300 foot-tons of energy to each able-bodied male, 3000 to each horse, and 4000 to each horse-power of steam-engines—we find the following result as the sum of the industrial power of mankind:—

	Million Foot-tons Daily.				Foot-tons per Inhabitant.	Per Centage of Steam.
	Hand.	Horse.	Steam.	Total.		
Great Britain	2,310	8,700	38,960	49,970	1,380	78
France	2,970	8,500	16,150	27,620	720	58
Germany	3,330	10,100	19,800	33,230	716	60
Russia	6,300	48,600	6,340	61,240	710	10
Austria	2,850	11,300	5,800	19,950	520	29
Italy	2,160	2,040	2,220	6,420	230	34
Spain	1,260	1,980	2,210	5,450	340	41
Portugal	360	210	280	850	205	34
Switzerland	210	330	1,300	1,840	670	71
Belgium	420	850	3,410	4,680	880	73
Holland	300	840	920	2,060	502	45
Scandinavia	630	2,900	1,830	5,360	630	34
Europe	23,100	96,350	99,220	218,670	706	45
United States	3,480	32,100	42,160	77,740	1,440	54
Total	26,580	128,450	141,380	296,410	802	48
Europ. Continent	20,790	87,650	60,260	168,700	610	36

Thus we see that nearly half the world's work is done by steam, the countries in which this agent performs the largest share of daily labour being Great Britain, Belgium, and Switzerland, a long way after which come Germany, France, and United States. The last-mentioned country, however, has so large a number of horses that this is precisely what makes its *ratio* of work done by steam less than in some other countries. The steam-power of the United States is 8 per cent. greater than that of the United Kingdom, and constitutes more than one-fourth of that of the world, and the ratio of energy per inhabitant is double that of the average European, being even 4 per cent. over that of an Englishman. The immense difference between the industrial power of nations appears in the fact that the united labour of 6 English and 6 Americans is equal to that of 24 French or Germans, 32 Austrians, 50 Spaniards, 75 Italians, or 84 Portuguese. The French or German may be fully as dexterous and possibly better educated than our workman, but the inadequate supply of machinery puts all Continental nations at a considerable disadvantage compared with Great Britain. So long as we do 80 per cent. of all our daily work by steam, which is the cheapest mode of industry, and that Continental nations accomplish only 36 per cent. by the same agency, the pre-eminence of this country in manufactures is nowise in danger.

If we take the number of able-bodied men and allow them the current workman's wages in each country, add to this the cost of feeding the horses, and put down steam at one shilling per horse-power daily, we can arrive at the total sum of daily expenditure for industry and the cost of 1000 foot-tons of energy in each country as follows:—

LABOUR AND ENERGY.

A. *Foot-tons of Energy obtained for £1 Sterling.*

28,520	24,480	23,890	23,520	21,470	20,730	19,040	17,420	17,110	18,320	14,970	13,440
G. Britain.	U. States.	Belgium.	Scandinavia.	Switzerland.	Germany.	Russia.	Spain.	France.	Holland.	Austria.	Italy.

B. *Proportion of Steam, Horse, and Hand Labour.*

G. Britain. Belgium. Switzerland. Germany. France. U. States. Holland. Spain. Italy. Scandinavia. Austria. Russia.

Steam, thus —☐   Horse, thus —☐   Hand, thus —■

	Daily Cost of Industry, 000's omitted.				Cost of 1000 Foot-tons Energy. Pence.	Workman's Wage, Pence Daily.
	Hand. £	Horse. £	Steam. £	Total. £		
Great Britain	970	360	487	1,817	8·4	30
France	1,105	350	202	1,657	14·2	26
Germany	920	420	247	1,587	11·6	20
Russia	1,040	2,100	80	3,220	12·6	12
Austria	800	470	70	1,340	16·1	20
Italy	360	85	30	475	17·8	12
Spain	205	80	30	315	13·8	12
Portugal	60	10	5	75	21·2	12
Switzerland	60	10	15	85	11·2	20
Belgium	120	35	43	198	10·1	20
Holland	80	35	11	126	14·7	20
Scandinavia	130	120	23	273	10·2	15
Europe	5,850	4,075	1,243	11,168	12·1	18
United States	1,950	1,360	527	3,837	9·8	40
Total	7,800	5,435	1,770	15,005	12·0	21
European Continent	4,880	3,715	756	9,351	13·3	16

We see that 1000 foot-tons of energy in Great Britain cost 8½d., or 1½d. less than in United States, and 5d. less than the Continental average, notwithstanding the fact that our workmen earn almost double the Continental wages. Now, energy is only another term for work, which represents ordinarily one-third of the value of any article; and as energy costs 36 per cent. less in Great Britain than on the Continent, it follows that we can, *cæteris paribus*, turn out our merchandise 12 per cent. cheaper than the Continental average. This margin of itself would enable us to fight the hostile tariffs of many foreign countries, and there can be no doubt that it does so.

The working-power of Europe and United States has increased as follows:—

Year.	Hand.	Horse.	Steam.	Total.	Foot-tons per Inhab.
		Energy, Million Foot-tons daily.			
1850	20,160	102,700	25,260	148,120	527
1860	22,104	112,200	45,600	179,904	595
1870	24,192	117,300	78,160	219,652	660
1880	26,580	128,450	115,780	270,810	750
1885	27,830	134,900	140,400	303,130	802

Since 1850 population has risen 34, working-power 105, per cent., and as a consequence five men can now accomplish as much as six in 1870 or eight in 1850. Thus, to go back no further than 1870, there has been an economy of labour equal to 17 per cent., which necessarily involves a reduction of 6 per cent in the value of all commodities. And as steam-power is increasing at the rate of 20,000 horse weekly, which adds 80 million foot-tons daily to the power of industry, we may expect a further saving of 15 per cent. in labour in the next ten years, which will cause a fall of 5 per cent. in market-prices, unless unforeseen calamities come to arrest the tendency to a lower price-level.

Mechanical inventions are closely connected with steam-power, and have introduced still more remarkable economy of labour. In 1880 there were known to be 5 million sewing-machines at work, doing as much labour as 60 million women could do with the needle. There were also 3100 Boston bootmaking machines in various parts of the world, turning out 150 million pairs of boots yearly, one man being able with this machine to produce from 240 to 300 pairs daily. These two inventions have greatly reduced the cost of clothing and of boots and shoes. Agricultural machinery has effected a similar saving of labour. In fact, there is no branch of industry that has not in recent years felt the benefits resulting from mechanical invention and cheapness of production.

The points worthy of notice in this chapter are :—

First. That the world's steam-power is now five and a half times what it was in 1850, and has nearly doubled since 1870.

Secondly. That the industrial power of nations between hand, horse, and steam is now 802 foot-tons per inhabitant, against 527 in 1850, and that consequently five men can perform as much work as eight could about thirty years ago.

Thirdly. That this involves a saving of 40 per cent. since 1850 in labour, which necessitates a fall of 13 per cent. in price, unless counteracted by other causes.

Fourthly. That steam-power is increasing 20,000 horse *weekly*, and hence further economy and another fall in price.

Fifthly. That energy costs $8\frac{1}{2}$d. per 1000 foot-tons in Great Britain, 10d. in United States, and $13\frac{1}{2}$d. on the Continent.

Sixthly. That this advantage enables us, as far as labour is concerned, to undersell Continental nations by 12 per cent., although our workmen's wages are almost double.

Seventhly. That, comparing energy with population, ten English or Americans are equal to twenty French or Germans, twenty-six Austrians, forty Spaniards, sixty Italians, or sixty-eight Portuguese, even though the foreigners in question be as intelligent as our people.

Eighthly. That no country does so large a proportion of its work (78 per cent.) by steam as Great Britain.

Ninthly. That the United States possess absolutely more steam-power ($10\frac{1}{2}$ million horse) than any other country, Great Britain coming second.

Tenthly. That steam and machinery powerfully aid each other in economising labour and reducing prices to a lower level.

X.

TEXTILE MANUFACTURES.

ONE of the principal reasons for the fall in price-level is the unprecedented development of manufactures, especially textiles. While the population of Europe, United States, and British Colonies has risen 34 per cent. since 1850, the consumption of fibre has risen 137 per cent., as shown in the following table :—

	Millions of Pounds.			
Year.	Cotton.	Wool.	Flax, Jute, &c.	Total.
1850	1,302	836	1,640	3,778
1860	2,391	1,021	1,690	5,102
1870	2,474	1,426	1,870	5,770
1880	4,039	1,652	2,154	7,845
1883	4,778	1,716	2,540	9,034

The downward movement of prices has extended the sphere of consumption, and it seems that if the world were to produce double the present quantity of textile raw material there would still be millions of purchasers for the manufactured stuffs, equal to the utmost capacity of production, provided prices were low enough to come within their reach. Thus the largest consumption is of cotton goods, because they are cheaper than linens or woollens.

The cotton crop of the world has quadrupled since 1850, viz. :—

TEXTILE MANUFACTURES.

Million Pounds.

Year.	United States.	India.	Egypt, &c.	Total.
1850	890	310	102	1,302
1860	1,870	420	101	2,391
1870	1,540	625	309	2,474
1880	3,161	540	338	4,039
1883	3,610	830	338	4,778

The value of the crop in 1883 was 90 millions sterling, and that of the manufactured goods 302 millions, including 95 millions for Great Britain. During the American war, in 1864, raw cotton went up to 28d. per pound, or five times its normal value, but calico did not rise in proportion, seldom reaching 6d. a yard, or double its ordinary price. The consumption of raw cotton among the factories of all nations is shown as follows:—

	Millions of lbs.				Ratio.	
	1850.	1860.	1870.	1883.	1850.	1883.
Great Britain	588	1,140	1,101	1,487	45·2	31·0
United States	225	434	530	1,080	17·3	22·6
Germany	170	220	260	372	13·0	7·8
France	163	215	250	253	12·5	5·3
Other countries	156	382	333	1,586	12·0	33·3
	1,302	2,391	2,474	4,778	100·0	100·0

Notwithstanding the fall of prices, cotton-factories constitute one of the elements of our national wealth. The following table shows the sums paid for raw cotton since 1850, the value of goods manufactured, and the net result:—

	Millions sterling.			
Years.	Raw Cotton.	Manufactures.	Net Result.	Ratio of Result.
1851–60	241	579	338	58 per cent.
1861–70	428	760	332	44 ,,
1871–83	507	1,225	718	59 ,,

Since 1870 the net result has averaged 55 millions sterling per annum, which is distributed between wages, sundry expenses, and profit on capital. This net result, compared with the total earnings of the nation, is about 4½ per cent.

Wool has more than doubled since 1850, that is, the increase has been three times faster than that of population, the clip of all nations summing up as follows :—

	Million lbs.			
	1850.	1860.	1870.	1883.
Europe	630	715	807	660
United States	90	112	154	208
River Plate	25	56	167	305
Australia	43	70	197	421
Cape Colony	48	68	101	122
Total	836	1,021	1,426	1,716

The nominal weight of wool is much in excess of the reality, owing to the presence of grease and dirt, which average 30 per cent in Cape wool, 45 in Australia, and 70 per cent. in the River Plate. The annual production may therefore be said not to exceed 1100 million lbs., or something less than one-fourth of the weight of cotton.

It is remarkable that the price of woollen manufactures in Great Britain has not declined in the same manner as that of the raw material, which appears from the following table :—

	Wool Consumed.		Manufactures, Millions £.			Value of	
Year.	Pence per lb.	Million lbs.	Export.	Home.	Total.	Wool.	Manufacture.
1850	23	158	10·1	19.6	29·7	100	100
1860	20	224	16·0	21·5	37·5	87	88
1870	15	309	31·4	23·3	54·7	65	94
1883	12	328	21·6	24·0	45·6	52	74

Unless there be special reasons to the contrary, this industry must leave sufficient margin for good profits, seeing that the value of manufactured woollens, according to weight, has fallen only 26 per cent. since 1850, while wool has declined 48 per cent. The following table shows the ratio between raw material and woollens at different periods :—

TEXTILE MANUFACTURES. 61

| | Millions £. | | Ratio. | |
Year.	Cost of Wool.	Value of Manufacture.	Wool to	Manufacture.
1850	15·2	29·7	100	195
1860	18·6	37·5	100	202
1870	19·4	54·7	100	281
1883	16·4	45·6	100	277

The reason of the relative change of value between wool and manufactured goods is, that wages have not fallen, but the reverse, and hence the raw material comes to form in comparison a smaller item in the cost of production. The Franco-German War in 1870 appears to have enhanced the value of woollen fabrics, most of the French and German mills having been in a manner paralysed for the time being.

Linen is an industry that seems threatened with extinction, the area under flax in Europe having diminished 710,000 acres, that is, 20 per cent., since 1866-70. Moreover, the consumption in Great Britain is now only four yards per inhabitant, showing a decline of one-half since 1850, viz :—

| | Million Yards. | | | Home Use. |
Year.	Made.	Exported.	Home Use.	Yards per Inhab.
1850	344	120	244	8·2
1860	290	144	146	5·1
1870	413	223	190	6·0
1883	306	159	147	4·1

The price of linen since 1881 has been 7 per cent. below the mean average for thirty preceding years, but a fall in price has no effect in widening the market for consumption, this fabric being more than twice as dear as cotton goods, which are, therefore, preferred.

Jute is a newly developed industry, India being the great producer and Great Britain the principal seat of manufacture, viz :—

	Million lbs.		Manufacture	
Year.	Export from India.	Consumed in Great Britain.	Value. Millions £.	Pence per Yard.
1850	43	42	0·9	7·2
1860	84	86	1·9	4·6
1870	264	324	9·5	3·6
1880	670	407	8·6	3·0
1883	804	618	11·7	2·6

Silk, by reason of its costly nature, has not made such progress as the coarser fibres, the consumption of all nations being now 38 million lbs., against 30 million in 1850.

The total value of textile manufactures in the world has been as follows:—

	Millions Sterling.				Ratio.	
	1850.	1860.	1870.	1883.	1850.	1883.
Cottons	92	166	210	302	100	328
Woollens	151	172	220	223	100	149
Silks	52	60	70	73	100	140
Linens, Jute, &c.	55	61	67	70	100	127
All textiles	350	459	567	668	100	191

Thus it appears that the value of textile manufactures is now 91 per cent. over the year 1850, while the weight of raw material consumed shows an advance of 137 per cent.

The consumption of all kinds of fibre in the United Kingdom is shown in the following table:—

	Million lbs.				Ratio.	
	1850.	1860.	1870.	1883.	1850.	1883.
Cotton	565	1,140	1,101	1,487	100	263
Wool	158	224	309	328	100	208
Flax	249	228	291	230	100	92
Hemp	122	78	160	170	100	140
Jute	42	86	324	618	100	1,471
Total	1,136	1,756	2,185	2,833	100	250

The consumption has grown much faster than population,

TEXTILE MANUFACTURES. 63

having averaged 41 lbs. in 1850 and 80 lbs. in 1883, a strong proof of the flourishing nature of our textile industries.

The points deserving special notice in this chapter are :—

First. That the world has an unlimited demand for textile fabrics, and that the power of consumption extends not in ratio with the fall of price, but in much wider degree.

Secondly. That a decline of 11 per cent. all round in price has caused consumption to increase 137 per cent. since 1850.

Thirdly. That while cheaper goods, such as cotton and jute manufactures, are every day finding wider markets, linen is in decadence.

Fourthly. That the rise or fall of raw material affects the price of manufactured goods in a diminished ratio.

Fifthly. That in spite of (or rather because of) lower price-level, the net proceeds of British cotton manufactures have been much higher since 1870 than at any former period.

Sixthly. That the textile manufactures of the world have advanced 91 per cent. in value since 1850, and the weight of goods 137 per cent., showing an apparent fall of 20 per cent. in price-level.

Seventhly. That the real fall in price has been only 11 per cent., as shown by comparing the market values in 1883 with what the same volume of goods would have brought if prices had not fallen, viz. :—

	Millions Sterling.		Ratio.	
	Value in 1883.	At Prices of 1850.	Value in 1883.	Price of 1850.
Cotton goods	302	339	89	100
Woollen ,,	223	262	85	100
Silk ,,	73	66	110	100
Linen, jute, &c.	70	85	82	100
Total	668	752	89	100

XI.

HARDWARE AND SUNDRIES.

IRON being the raw material of most hardware, we see what enormous development this branch of manufactures has had, the production of this metal having almost quintupled between 1850 and 1882; that is to say, it has increased three times faster than fibre, and twelve times than population, the figures being as follows:—

	Tons, 000's omitted.			Pounds per Inhabitant.		
	1850.	1870.	1882.	1850.	1870.	1882.
Great Britain	2,250	5,230	8,488	190	420	555
United States	560	1,580	4,023	54	90	196
Germany	402	1,310	3,171	26	82	140
France	408	1,230	2,033	25	83	117
Belgium	170	260	640	85	115	250
Austria	140	280	550	11	17	30
Russia	220	360	505	8	11	12
Sweden	130	300	410	84	165	190
Total	4,280	10,550	19,820	42	90	150

Such is the magnitude of this industry that we consume 1½ lb. of iron daily per inhabitant in the United Kingdom, including what is made into steel. The inventions of Bessemer and Siemens have so completely altered the relative value of steel and iron, that whereas twenty years ago a ton of the former was worth eleven tons of the latter, the proportion now is barely four to one. We find that the production of steel has increased seventy-fold since 1850, being now extensively used instead of iron, not only for domestic

HARDWARE AND SUNDRIES.

purposes, but also for rails and shipbuilding. The consumption of iron and steel and the value of manufactures, at the accepted standard of £8 per ton for iron and £50 for steel merchandise, are shown as follows:—

	Tons Used, 000's omitted.		Value, Millions Sterling.		
	Iron.	Steel.	Iron.	Steel.	Total.
Great Britain	4,890	1,780	39	89	128
United States	3,700	1,460	30	73	103
Germany	1,500	900	12	45	57
France	1,600	420	13	21	34
Belgium	570	135	6	7	13
Austria	320	180	3	9	12
Russia	260	300	2	15	17
Other countries	1,200	200	10	10	20
	14,040	5,375	115	266	384

Railways take two-thirds of all the steel that is made, as shown in this table:—

	Tons Steel Rails, 000's omitted.		
	New Lines.	Renewal.	Total.
Great Britain	60	160	220
Continent, &c.	680	655	1,335
United States	1,200	900	2,100
Total	1,940	1,715	3,655

Steel rails are found to last twice as long as iron ones; in December 1882 the existing railways of the world had 14 million tons steel and 20 million tons iron, rails; but the latter were being removed, to make way for steel.

Great Britain owes much of her manufacturing ascendancy to the cheap production of iron and steel. The average prices of iron during ten years ending 1880 were, 68s. per ton in England, 88 on the Continent, and 116 shillings in the United States. The "protective" duties in the United States added 75 per cent. to the price of pig-iron; in ten years (1871–80) the American people paid 203 millions sterling for 35 million tons, which they could have obtained from England, delivered in New York, for the sum of 133 millions: the difference added seriously to the cost of making new railways in that country. According to a report by the French Government to the Chambers, neither France nor Germany can compete with England or Belgium for cheapness of production, the cost being as follows:—

	Shillings per Ton.		
	Pig Iron.	Wrought Iron.	Steel.
Belgium	47	130	131
England	50	122	160
Germany	59	144	192
France	73	182	224

Shipbuilding is one of the industries most intimately connected with iron and steel, and at present Great Britain builds two-thirds of all the shipping of the world, the tonnage having risen thus:—

	Tons Shipping Built, 000's omitted.				Ratio.	
	1850.	1860.	1870.	1882.	1850.	1882.
Great Britain	134	212	343	1,194	21·3	66·2
United States	272	213	277	281	43·2	15·6
Various	224	545	720	330	35·5	18·2
Total	630	970	1,340	1,805	100·0	100·0

In 1882 the total value of shipping built was 30 millions sterling, for 1,200,000 tons of steamers and 600,000 tons sailing. The largest merchant vessel recently built is the Umbria, by John Elder & Co., 8000 tons and 12,000 horse-power; but she is surpassed by the Italian war steamer Lepanto, 14,600 tons and 18,000 horse-power. Ironclads cost from £50 to £60 per ton. The average of steel vessels built on the Clyde since 1881 has exceeded 100,000 tons per annum, ships made of this material being able to carry 20 per cent. more than iron ones.

Timber constitutes another great industry, representing an

annual value of 273 millions sterling: consumption has increased 50 per cent since 1850, viz.:—

	Millions, Cubic Feet.		Value in 1881. Millions Sterling.	Cubic Feet per Inhab.
	1850.	1881.		
Great Britain	205	430	20·2	12
France	960	1,280	21·4	33
Germany	1,100	1,450	24·5	32
Russia	4,200	6,120	56·3	76
Austria	1,400	1,880	30·1	51
Italy, Spain, &c.	1,200	1,605	37·7	23
Europe	9,065	12,765	190·2	41
United States	1,400	3,100	77·4	58
Canada	100	220	5·4	49
The World	10,565	16,085	273·0	44

Firewood takes 48 per cent. of the total, the rest being used for building, carpentry, cabinet-work, and other purposes. The supply of timber being practically inexhaustible, there has been a fall of 36 per cent. in the price, notwithstanding the rapid increase of consumption. The forests of the world cover 1200 million acres, viz.:—

	Million Acres.
Russia	485
United States	176
Canada	174
Brazil	135
Other countries	232
	1,202

The area annually felled by woodcutters is only 19 million acres, and may be increased to 40 million before reaching the annual average increase of forest-trees. Russia, for example, can afford to cut two and a half times the amount of her present consumption without impairing her capital in trees. There is, therefore, no ground for the alarm that our posterity in the next century may have to pay famine prices for timber; on the contrary, we may look for a continued fall in prices, as facilities increase for conveying timber cheaply to the seaports of the world.

Leather has not grown so fast as other manufactures, because cows and horses cannot be multiplied with the same facility as agricultural or mineral products. It has just kept a little ahead of the growth of population in Europe and North America, the consumption and value of manufactures being as follows :—

	Leather, Million Lbs.		Manufactures, Millions £.	
	1855.	1881.	1855.	1881.
Great Britain . .	130	209	24·3	34·0
Continent . .	420	490	79·0	85·0
United States . .	110	215	20·0	37·0
Other countries .	105	160	19·5	28·0
Total .	765	1,074	142·8	184·0

Notwithstanding the limited production, there has been a fall of 11 per cent. since 1850, and a still greater reduction in the cost of boots and shoes, owing to the introduction of improved machinery. The statistics of the British leather trade are summed up as follows :—

Year.	Leather, Million Lbs.			Manufactures, Millions £.			Lbs. Leather per Inhab.
	British Hide.	Foreign Hide.	Total.	Home.	Export.	Total.	
1850 . .	50	70	120	19·7	0·6	20·3	4·4
1860 . .	55	87	142	22·3	2·1	24·4	5·0
1870 . .	60	132	192	28·6	2·6	31·2	6·1
1881 . .	65	144	209	30·1	3·9	34·0	6·0

Although many substitutes for leather have been introduced, thus relieving the demand for hides, there are good reasons to suppose that a higher range of prices may be expected; the value of land and cattle is rising in America and Australia, and hides must rise also.

Books are not always classified among manufactures, and yet constitute an industry of great importance, the annual value (including journals) amounting to 79 millions sterling.

HARDWARE AND SUNDRIES.

The following table shows the consumption of printing-paper and the annual amount expended in various nations for books and newspapers:—

	Per Annum.			
	Million Lbs. Paper.	Lbs. per Inhabitant.	Value of Books, &c., Millions £.	Pence per Inhabitant.
United Kingdom	220	6·1	16·2	107
France	160	4·2	11·8	75
Germany	170	3·7	12·7	67
Russia	40	0·5	3·1	9
Austria	54	1·4	4·1	25
Italy	43	1·5	3·2	26
Spain and Portugal	17	0·8	1·4	15
Belgium and Holland	27	2·7	2·0	48
Scandinavia	13	1·5	1·0	30
Switzerland	9	3·2	0·7	58
Europe	753	2·4	56·2	40
United States	262	4·6	19·0	75
Canada	10	2·2	0·7	39
Australia	9	3·3	0·7	52
Spanish America	24	0·9	1·7	14
India, &c.	12	...	1·0	...
The World	1,070	...	79·3	...

The above shows an average value of 18d. per lb. of books, or £168 per ton, but the customs-value for those exported from England in 1881–84 was only £97 per ton, which must have been much below the real value. In some countries the customs tariff is 5 francs per kilogramme, or about 2s. per lb. As regards consumption of printing-paper to population, the ratio is much higher in Great Britain than elsewhere, and the average expenditure on books and newspapers nearly 9s. a head. The price of books in England has declined 32 per cent. since 1860, according to customs valuation.

The principal points of this chapter are these:—

First. That the consumption of iron, with regard to population, is now four times as much as it was in 1850 in Europe and United States.

Secondly. That steel is now produced at one-third the cost of twenty years ago.

Thirdly. That Great Britain and Belgium produce iron and steel cheaper than other countries.

Fourthly. That the felling of timber is far less than the growth, and that the fall in prices since 1850 is likely to continue.

Fifthly. That the fall in leather will probably be checked before long by the rise in land and cattle in the Colonies.

Sixthly. That books have fallen one-third in price since 1860, and that Great Britain consumes one-fifth of the printing-paper of the world.

XII.

MINING.

THIS great industry, which employs nearly 2½ million men, represents an annual product of 244 millions sterling, the precious metals forming only 14 per cent. of the total. The annual value of all minerals produced is three times greater than in 1850; the actual weight extracted has quadrupled, being now 402 million tons, against 101 million. The following table shows the value at pit's mouth at various dates :—

	Value, Millions Sterling.				Ratio.	
	1850.	1860.	1870.	1883.	1850.	1883.
Gold	12·7	22·8	23·9	18·2	100	144
Silver	8·1	9·6	14·5	15·9	100	196
Coal	35·5	67·2	98·6	136·4	100	384
Sundries	31·0	38·3	51·5	73·3	100	237
Total	87·3	137·9	188·5	243·8	100	279

The production and uses of gold and silver have been already alluded to in Chap. III., on the Precious Metals, but there are some points in connection with mining which deserve further notice. In California 3,300,000 gold-diggers extracted 148 million tons ore, from which they obtained 2106 tons of fine gold, that is, a little over 70,000 tons ore for 1 ton of gold. In Australia 3,270,000 diggers extracted 183 million tons ore, from which they got 1940 tons gold, that is, 94,000 tons ore for 1 ton of gold. The Californian took out 45 tons, the Australian 56 tons, of ore yearly, but the former averaged 10 per cent. more gold than the latter, the Californian ore being 30 per cent. richer. Nevertheless, the largest nugget was found in Australia, the Ballarat Welcome (11th June 1858) yielding 2020 oz. gold, worth £8380 sterling. About 5 per cent. of the gold-diggers, say 330,000, died of exposure or violence, and the value of gold divided among the rest averaged 6s. a day, which was sometimes less than the price of a dozen eggs. American economists say that every £ sterling of precious metals dug out of the earth since 1850 has cost 24s. The ore extracted by the miners would suffice to raise ninety pyramids like that of Cheops, and yet all the gold produced by California and Australia together would fit in a drawing-room ten yards long, seven wide, and five in height.

The quantity of fine silver extracted since 1850 has been 53,000 tons, or thirteen times that of gold; but as the latter was then fifteen and a half times as valuable as the former, it is plain that the production of silver has not kept pace with that of gold, a fact ignored by bi-metallists.

Coal stands for 55 per cent. of the total value of minerals. The production has quadrupled, viz. :—

Year.			Million Tons.			British Ratio.
			British.	Foreign.	Total.	
1850	.	.	48	40	88	55 per cent.
1860	.	.	80	61	141	57 ,,
1870	.	.	110	98	208	53 ,,
1883	.	.	160	220	380	52 ,,

This mineral plays so important a part in the majority of industries that its increased production has tended to a lower level of prices in most commodities, especially manufactured goods. The consumption averages 4 tons per inhabitant yearly in Great Britain, against 1½ ton in United States or Germany, 14 cwt. in France, and 2 cwt. in Russia or Italy. The statistics of production in 1880 were as follows :—

MINING.

	Millions of Tons.	Miners, 000's omitted.	Tons per Miner.	Value, Millions Sterling.	Per Ton, Shillings.
Great Britain	147	485	303	47·0	6·5
France	19	102	190	10·2	10·7
Germany	59	220	270	13·7	4·5
Austria	16	83	192	4·2	5·2
Belgium	17	101	168	6·1	7·2
United States	70	240	295	28·0	8·0
Russia, &c.	16	100	160	4·0	5·0
Total	344	1,331	258	113·2	6·6

Great Britain exports 24 million tons, or 15 per cent. of the quantity raised in the United Kingdom. The above values are at the pit's mouth, the retail price for consumers being twice or three times as much. Coal is dearer on the Continent, the above official values being under the reality.

Ironstone comes next after coal in bulk, the annual yield being now 52 million tons, against 27 million in 1870, and 11 million in 1850. The percentage of iron varies, the richest ore being that of Canada, viz. :—

Percentage of Iron in Ironstone.

France	31	United States	43	Australia	55
Germany	36	Russia	44	Algeria	58
England	41	Sweden	52	Canada	60

Before the invention of Neilson's hot-blast it took 5 tons of coal to produce a ton of pig-iron, and even thirty years ago the average was $3\frac{1}{2}$ tons; but Cowper's Regenerator (1500 Fahr.), invented in 1857, made a further economy of fuel, reducing the consumption to less that $2\frac{1}{2}$ tons. Thus the various ironworks in the world consume about 50 million tons coal to make 20 million tons pig-iron; in other words, a ton of iron represents $2\frac{1}{2}$ tons ironstone and $2\frac{1}{2}$ tons coal. When charcoal is used, 1 ton suffices to make a ton of iron.

Lead and copper are minerals of secondary importance, the production of which seems to surpass requirements; both have fallen 40 to 50 per cent. since 1850, and the tendency still looks downward. The production has been as follows of fine metal:—

	Thousands of Tons.				Value in Millions £.	
	Lead.		Copper.			
	1850.	1880.	1850.	1884.	Lead.	Copper.
Great Britain	55	51	12	3	0·8	0·2
France	7	32	2	5	0·5	0·3
Germany	16	59	2	15	1·0	0·8
Italy	12	33	...	2	0·5	0·1
Spain	27	92	1	41	1·5	2·1
Austria, &c.	17	23	9	14	0·4	0·7
Europe	134	290	26	80	4·7	4·2
United States	36	89	3	64	1·5	3·2
Chili	...	...	14	41	...	2·1
Australia	...	...	2	14	...	0·7
Japan and Cape	...	...	2	11	...	0·6
Total	170	379	47	210	6·2	10·8

Owing to the great increase of lead production in Spain and United States, some of the Austro-Hungarian mines have been closed. The Missouri lead-mines near Chicago give an ore containing 70 per cent. of metal, and those of Cordoba, Spain, are said to be even richer. Copper ores in 1850-55 used to give 6 per cent. of fine copper, but now they average 7 per cent., owing to the superior richness of the United States, Australian, and Chilian ores. Seeing that 6 tons of ore now give as much copper as 7 tons formerly, we may presume a saving of 14 per cent. in the cost of production, which would partly account for the fall in price. American copper averages a yield of 18, Australian of 12, per cent., against 7 per cent. British.

Tin is an inferior mineral, the value of which hardly exceeds 2½ millions sterling, the total production being 53,000 tons, viz. :—

	Tons.		Percentage of Metal.
	Tin Ore.	Tin Metal.	
Australia	24,100	17,500	74
Great Britain	13,700	9,200	66
Java	15,000	9,000	60
Total	52,800	35,700	69

Great Britain consumes 60 per cent. of all that is produced, the average of our tin manufactures being now 22 ounces per inhabitant, against 10 ounces in 1850; prices have fallen 10 per cent. in twenty years.

Zinc is another mineral of little note, the value not reaching three millions sterling. Prussia produces 102,000 tons of this metal, or 60 per cent. of the total. About 6 tons of ore give a ton of metallic zinc. The manufacture of this metal in Great Britain reaches 52,000 tons, having trebled in the last fifteen years.

Mercury is produced to the amount of 3340 tons, worth £700,000, California giving 60 per cent., Spain 30 per cent., of the total; the consumption in Great Britain averages 1600 tons.

Diamond-mining occupies a small number of negroes near Bahia, Brazil, who produce about £100,000 worth yearly. The diamond-fields of Cape Colony were discovered in 1867, and have produced stones to the value of 30 millions sterling, the annual product since 1878 having been £3,450,000; there were in 1884 about 10,000 Basutos and 8000 whites at the diggings; the Stewart diamond, found in November 1872, weighed 288 carats, and was sold for £11,000 sterling. The average earnings at the diamond-fields have for some years been £180 per miner, or double that of the gold-diggers in Australia.

Petroleum or mineral oil is a most valuable product, and was first discovered in Pennsylvania in 1859, since which

76 HISTORY OF PRICES.

time the oil-wells have yielded 11,570 million gallons, representing a value of 303 millions sterling, at a medium of 6d. per gallon, viz. :—

Years.	Millions of Gallons per Annum.			Value of Product. Millions £.	Pence per Gallon.
	Produced.	Home Use.	Exported.		
1859-63	60	54	6	5·7	22
1864-68	130	82	48	9·3	17
1869-73	320	187	133	11·6	9
1874-80	680	340	340	13·7	5
1881-84	1,065	577	488	17·7	4

The consumption in the United States has risen from 2 gallons in 1860 to 11 gallons in 1884 per inhabitant. The enormous increase of production has brought a great reduction of price, the number of wells actually working being over 6000, at depths ranging from 400 to 1200 feet.

If we sum up all the mining industries of the world, we find as follows (1883) :—

	Miners, 000's omitted.	Minerals. Millions £.	Product. £ per Miner.
Great Britain	538	79	146
France	206	14	70
Germany	231	19	82
Russia	207	10	48
Austria	92	8	86
Italy	32	2	52
Spain	70	6	86
Belgium	110	7	62
Sweden	29	1	35
United States	560	77	140
Spanish America	150	10	66
Australia	95	8	84
Other countries	66	3	47
The World	2,390	244	102

The principal points of this chapter are these :—

First. That the production of coal is four times as valuable as that of gold and silver in the aggregate.

Secondly. That gold and silver mining are among the least profitable industries.

Thirdly. That a saving of 33 per cent. in coal since 1857 for reducing ironstone to pig-iron is equivalent to a fall of 11 per cent. in the price of iron.

Fourthly. That the richer quality of copper ores now worked involves a saving of 14 per cent. in the production of that metal.

Fifthly. That petroleum, which stands for 7 per cent. of the total value of mining products in the world, has fallen 80 per cent. in price in twenty years.

Sixthly. That the general decline of prices for minerals, either by reason of reduced cost of production or because the supply is excessive, has caused a downward tendency in most other products.

Seventhly. That mining industry represents a value of 244 millions, or nearly 5 per cent. of the annual products of human labour.

XIII.

AGRICULTURE.

NOTWITHSTANDING the great development of agriculture (under which are also included all pastoral pursuits), there has been a rise of prices, which, as we shall see later on, amounts to 11 per cent. over the level of 1841–50; whereas in the same period the price-level of manufactures has declined exactly 25 per cent. This is the more surprising as we have to record a fall of 7 per cent. in grain, which constitutes two-fifths of the total, besides a decline of 43 per cent. in sugar and 48 per cent. in wool; but all other items have risen, as appears from the following table of ratios:—

	1841–50.	1851–60.	1861–70.	1871–80.	1881–84.
Grain	100	121	117	109	93
Meat	100	112	118	133	148
Dairy products	100	112	128	141	144
Potatoes	100	109	134	143	157
Wine	100	122	130	130	151
Raw cotton	100	112	241	133	114
Wool	100	90	78	61	52
Sugar	100	94	100	79	57
Coffee	100	130	165	217	183
Tobacco	100	151	183	131	127
Tea	100	125	150	131	100
	1,100	1,278	1,544	1,408	1,326

There is a notable rise in seven articles, while three have fallen, since 1850; but the index numbers in the aggregate do not show the actual variations of price-level, for we find that the quantities of the above articles, according to consumption, which cost £100 in 1841–50, would now cost £111, and not £120, as would appear from the above totals. If we place the index numbers beside the actual variations, as measured by the trade-volume system, we find as follows:—

AGRICULTURE.

	Index Numbers.	Trade-Level.
1845–50	100	100
1851–60	116	116
1861–70	140	121
1871–80	128	117
1881–84	120	111

The weak point of the index numbers is seen, for example, in the fact that, in the preceding table, for the decade ending 1870 raw cotton weighs for twice as much as grain, whereas the "trade-level" gives grain 15 times the importance of raw cotton, viz., as 253 to 17 (see chap. xviii.).

The progress of agriculture since 1850 is first observable in the fact that the area under crops has risen 55 per cent., while population has increased only 34 per cent., viz.:—

	Million Acres.			Acres per Family.		
	1850.	1870.	1884.	1850.	1870.	1884.
Europe	360	440	482	7·3	7·4	7·4
United States	55	88	157	12·0	11·4	14·3
British Colonies	12	18	25	17·0	15·0	16·0
Total	427	546	664	7·8	8·2	8·5

Among the causes in Europe which stimulated rural industry have been the abolition of feudalism in Germany and Austria, the emancipation of Russian serfs, the construction of railways, and the use of agricultural machinery. In each succeeding decade since 1850 there has been in all countries a marked tendency of rural population to migrate to the towns; and although the rural ratio of inhabitants has seriously diminished, there has been an increase of tillage, in consequence of machinery displacing hand labour. The influx of immigrants into the United States has had a marked effect in that country, the area under crops having doubled.

Grain-growing constitutes the chief branch of tillage, covering an area of 505 million acres, and producing crops worth 1326 millions sterling, or one-fourth the value of the aggregate of human industries, viz.:—

	Millions of Acres.	Millions of Bushels.	Bushels per Acre.	Value of Crop, Millions £.	Pence per Bushel.
Wheat	154	2,146	14	520	59
Oats	86	1,794	21	205	27
Barley	47	819	17	133	39
Rye	115	1,408	12	232	39
Maize, &c.	103	2,300	22	236	24
	505	8,467	17	1,326	38

The weight of the grain-crop is 212 million tons, of which 194 are consumed by the countries in which produced, and 18 million tons exported to others of deficient supply, the carriage of grain forming nearly one-eighth of maritime commerce, as regards bulk. Production varies from 9 bushels per inhabitant in United Kingdom to 49 in United States; the average for Europe is 16½ bushels production and 18 consumption per inhabitant, including herein the grain used for food of cattle.

The production and consumption of all kinds of grain are as follows:—

	Production, Millions of Bushels.			Consumption, Millions of Bushels.	Per Inhabitant, Bushels.	
	Wheat.	Other Grain.	Total.		Production.	Consumption.
United Kingdom	73	248	321	618	9·0	17·3
France	272	454	726	895	20·4	25·3
Germany	94	540	634	750	14·1	16·7
Russia	210	1,500	1,710	1,500	20·8	18·0
Austria	115	433	548	516	14·8	13·9
Italy	140	153	293	298	10·7	10·9
Spain and Portugal	145	180	325	325	16·2	16·2
Belgium and Holland	24	81	105	145	11·1	15·5
Scandinavia	7	163	170	160	20·1	18·9
Roumania, &c.	85	140	225	205	32·1	29·3
Europe	1,165	3,892	5,057	5,412	16·8	18·0
United States	510	2,030	2,540	1,920	46·0	34·5
Canada	45	85	130	120	31·2	28·8
Australia	35	25	60	40	22·2	14·8
India	270	...	270	230	...	...
Other countries	121	289	410	745	...	...
Total	2,146	6,321	8,467	8,467	21·0	21·0

The benefits of improved agricultural implements are apparent in the fact that (omitting India) the average product of grain per inhabitant is now 21 bushels, against 20 in 1870 and 19 in 1850, while the number of persons actually engaged in agriculture seems less. But this improvement is susceptible of far greater development, the waste of labour in such countries as France or Belgium, owing to the smallness of the farms, or in Russia by reason of lack of machinery, being especially deplorable; the same amount of labour would be four or five times as productive under proper circumstances. The average product of grain to each able-bodied male peasant engaged in tillage in the various countries is as follows:—

Bushels, per Peasant.

United States	920	Germany	245	Spain	16
Great Britain	540	France	220	Russia	15
Canada	350	Austria	180	Italy	14

On this subject I take the following passage from Mr. Edward Atkinson's valuable work on the "Distribution of Products:"[1]—

"The equivalent of one man's work on the great farms of Dakota is 5500 bushels of wheat per annum, if the crop reach 20 bushels to the acre. Retaining enough for seed, this quantity suffices to make 1000 barrels of flour. It can be carried through the flour-mill and put into barrels, including the labour of making the barrel, at the equivalent of one other man's labour for one year; and at the ratio of the work done to each man employed upon the New York Central Railroad, the wheat can be moved from Dakota to a flour-mill in Minnesota, and thence the 1000 barrels of flour can be moved to the city of New York, and all the machinery

[1] Published in 1885 by Putnam's Sons, New York.

of the farm, the mill, and the railroad can be kept in repair at the equivalent of the labour of two more men; so that 1000 barrels of flour, the annual ration of 1000 people, can be placed in the city of New York from a point 2000 miles distant with the exertion of the human labour equivalent to that of only four men, working one year in producing, milling, and moving the wheat. It can there be baked and distributed by the work of three more persons; so that seven persons serve 1000 with bread."

There can be no doubt that if the peasant's labour in France, Germany, or Russia were as well ordered and productive as in the United States, the cost of grain in those countries would be less and the condition of 'the rural population improved. As all scientific inventions tend towards a lower price-level, we may conclude that grain has not yet touched what Jevons called "the minimum attainable cost of production." And as grain constitutes one-fourth of the value of all the industrial products of man, any further fall in its price must increase the purchasing power of gold. That is to say, if grain fall 8 per cent. by the year 1890, even though all other products and industries remain unchanged, the value of gold will rise 2 per cent.

All other forms of tillage are of minor note compared with grain; nevertheless wine-growing and potatoes considerably surpass the rest, together making up a value of 311 millions sterling. Detailed statistics of these and other agricultural products will be found in the Appendix.

Cattle-farming is closely allied to tillage, since cattle consume two-thirds of all the grain that is produced, and therefore must be included when treating of agriculture. The number of cows, sheep, and horses to population in the principal countries is as follows :—

AGRICULTURE.

	Per 100 Inhabitants.				Per 100 Inhabitants.		
	Cows.	Sheep.	Horses.		Cows.	Sheep.	Horses.
United Kingdom	28	80	8	Belgium	22	11	5
France	31	65	7	Denmark	70	90	18
Germany	34	55	7	Sweden	50	33	10
Russia	27	62	18	Roumania	37	67	6
Austria	34	56	10	Europe	29	63	10
Italy	12	25	2	U. States	77	90	20
Spain	19	145	4	Canada	60	75	19
Portugal	13	55	1	Australia	262	2,180	35
Holland	37	22	7	River Plate	613	2,540	205

The population of Europe has increased so fast in the last thirty years that the ratio of cattle to inhabitants has declined, which explains the rise in the price of meat. In 1855 there were 32 cows and 70 sheep for every 100 inhabitants, which numbers, compared with those for 1880, show that there has been a relative decline of 10 per cent., viz. :—

	Million Head.		Per 100 Inhabitants.	
	1855.	1880.	1855.	1880.
Cows	82·7	91·5	32	29
Sheep	181·4	194·2	70	63
Pigs	39·1	45·1	15	14

Meantime the number in the United States has doubled, but the increase of population has been so great that the ratio per inhabitant is no higher, viz. :—

	000's omitted.			Per 100 Inhabitants.	
	1850.	1870.	1883.	1850.	1880.
Cows	17,784	23,833	42,547	77	77
Sheep	21,722	28,481	50,627	94	90
Horses	4,331	7,155	11,170	19	20
Pigs	30,353	25,133	44,200	132	80

If it were not for the teeming pampas of the River Plate and the well-stocked farms of Australia, we might have reason to anticipate a great rise in the price of meat in Europe. In the United States there are not a cow and a sheep to each inhabitant, whereas in the River Plate there are 6 cows and 25 sheep. According to recent quotations at Buenos Ayres (August 1885), horned cattle were selling at 18 shillings, sheep 4 shillings, a head, which shows what a field of undeveloped meat-farming lies within fifteen days of Europe.

The following table shows the total agricultural capital of the various countries and the value of annual products :—

| | Millions Sterling. ||||||| Ratio per Inhab. ||
| | Capital. ||| Annual Product. |||| |
	Land.	Cattle, &c.	Total.	Crops.	Cattle.	Total.	Capital £	Product. £
United Kingdom	1,737	473	2,210	126	137	263	61	7·2
France	2,624	436	8,060	325	110	435	80	11·4
Germany	2,060	466	2,526	312	132	444	55	9·9
Russia	1,386	709	2,095	337	145	482	25	6·0
Austria	1,290	421	1,711	205	102	307	45	8·0
Italy	810	153	963	141	33	174	33	6·0
Spain	660	119	779	97	36	133	45	8·0
Portugal	158	37	195	24	6	30	46	7·0
Belgium	245	86	331	31	13	44	60	8·0
Holland	212	118	330	26	19	45	82	11·2
Denmark	210	59	269	23	14	37	135	18·5
Sweden	312	72	384	27	14	41	84	9·0
Norway	110	31	141	7	7	14	71	7·1
Greece	105	20	125	7	2	9	69	5·0
Europe	11,919	3,200	15,119	1,688	770	2,458	50	8·2
United States	2,116	845	2,961	346	198	544	54	10·1
Canada	180	79	259	31	21	52	57	11·6
Australia	182	136	318	37	39	76	106	24·7
Argentine Republic	105	103	208	11	23	34	69	11·3
Uruguay	16	27	43	1	4	5	90	11·0
Total	14,518	4,390	18,908	2,114	1,056	3,169	52	8·7

Some countries give a large return for the capital invested in agricultural pursuits, while others yield such poor profit as hardly to leave a margin for bad years or other drawbacks. Compare, for example, the following :—

High Returns.	Per Cent.	Low Returns.	Per Cent.
Australia	24	Belgium	13
Russia	23	Great Britain	12
Canada	20	Sweden	11
United States	18	Uruguay	11
Austria	18	Norway	10
Italy	18	Greece	7

In view of the above figures and the increase of agriculture in the newer parts of the world, we may expect a further decline of this industry in the countries comprised in the above column of "low returns," except Uruguay, where this industry will prove highly profitable as soon as things become more settled.

The principal points in this chapter are the following:—

First. That although the ratio of rural population has declined both in Europe and America, the area under tillage has risen 50 per cent., and the weight of crops in proportion.

Secondly. That grain-growing eclipses all other industries in point of value, and that any variation in price of grain seriously affects the purchasing power of gold.

Thirdly. That Europe has to import about 10 million tons of grain yearly from other parts of the globe.

Fourthly. That a farm-labourer in United States raises as much grain as four able-bodied French or Germans, or six Russians or Spaniards.

Fifthly. That consequently three-fourths of the labour of peasants on the Continent of Europe is in a manner wasted.

Sixthly. That we have not yet seen the lowest cost of production for grain in Europe.

Seventhly. That cattle to population are 10 per cent. fewer in Europe than thirty years ago, that the United States will require shortly all their own cows and sheep, and that Europe must look to Australia and the River Plate for a future supply of at least 1,200,000 tons of meat per annum.

Eighthly. That agriculture does not give profitable returns for the amount of capital invested in Sweden, Great Britain, or Belgium, and may therefore be expected steadily to decline in those countries, and give place to lucrative pursuits.

XIV.

FOOD-SUPPLY.

The food-supply of nations is the most important of all matters connected with price-level, since the money paid for food represents 45 per cent. of the earnings of mankind. Moreover, the margin that each country has for clothing and other merchandise depends on the relative amount of earnings absorbed by the cost of food, which may thus be said to regulate the consumption of all other commodities. In the following table are shown the values of food (1880–82) annually consumed by nations, excluding that which is eaten by cattle:—

	Millions Sterling.					Earnings, Millions Sterling.	Percentage Food to Earnings.
	Grain.	Meat.	Liquor.	Sundries.	Total.		
U. Kingdom	55	140	102	176	473	1,247	37·8
France	70	105	84	128	387	965	40·1
Germany	80	126	86	148	440	850	51·8
Russia	110	119	84	198	511	848	60·1
Austria	60	88	62	110	320	602	53·1
Italy	42	25	39	80	186	345	54·0
Spain	28	21	20	50	119	218	54·6
Belg. & Holl.	19	17	19	45	100	224	44·6
Scandinavia	15	15	13	31	74	151	49·0
U. States	85	110	74	265	534	1,420	37·6
Total	564	766	583	1,231	3,144	6,970	45·0

If we take the working year as 300 days, we find that food-supply requires the labour of 114 days in Great Britain or United States, 120 in France, 133 in Belgium and Holland, 155 in Germany, 162 in Italy, and 180 in Russia.

And if we compare the surplus of earnings over the cost of food per inhabitant, we find that an Englishman has £21, an American £17, a Frenchman £15, a German £9, an Italian £6, a Russian £4, their power of consumption varying according to the surplus.

All food may be classified under necessaries and sundries, the former comprising grain, meat, butter, cheese, sugar, and salt, which sum up an amount of 1620 millions sterling, or 52 per cent. of the total. Sundries include coffee, tea, tobacco, eggs, milk, fruit, vegetables, spices, &c.—in all, 1524 millions sterling. The total food expenditure for the above nations averages 6 pence a day per inhabitant, that is, 10 pence for a man, 8 pence for a woman, and 4 pence for a child. The averages are as follows:—

Pence per Inhabitant, Daily.

	Necessaries.	Sundries.	Total.		Necessaries.	Sundries.	Total.
Great Britain	5·0	4·0	9·0	Spain.	2·0	2·8	4·8
France	3·6	3·4	7·0	Belg. & Holl.	3·0	3·7	6·7
Germany	3·7	3·2	6·9	Denmark	3·6	3·7	7·3
Russia	2·1	2·0	4·1	Sweden	2·7	2·8	5·5
Austria	3·0	2·8	5·8	United States	3·4	3·6	7·0
Italy	1·8	2·6	4·4	Average	3·1	3·0	6·1

The sum of expenditure is no guide as to quantity, the American being the best fed, although his daily food costs 22 per cent. less than ours. According to the quantity and quality of food is the amount of work that each nation can do, or the number of foot-tons of energy that we can put forth. A fair day's work, whether of a mechanic, a letter-carrier, or a man writing essays, is 300 foot-tons, and the food requisite for such a worker should possess at least twelve times that force, or 3600 foot-tons of energy. As a matter of fact, the food consumed by different nations averages 5000 foot-tons per male adult, or 3000 per inhabitant, so that if there were no waste nobody should come short of food. The following table shows the foot-tons of energy in the various kinds of food: bread includes also potatoes;

dairy products comprise milk, butter, cheese and eggs; meat includes fish; and sundries are sugar, beer, &c. :—

	Foot-tons of Energy per Inhabitant Daily.					Average per Adult.	
	Bread.	Dairy.	Meat.	Sundries.	Total.	Male.	Female.
U. Kingdom	1,510	460	330	960	3,260	5,440	4,350
France	1,950	340	230	860	3,380	5,630	4,510
Germany	2,280	350	212	540	3,382	5,633	4,512
Russia	1,810	380	160	340	2,690	4,490	3,590
Austria	1,850	380	192	500	2,922	4,863	3,892
Italy	1,200	180	80	570	2,220	3,680	2,960
Spain	1,340	190	160	480	2,170	3,610	2,890
Belg. & Holl.	1,940	350	235	670	3,195	5,320	4,260
Scandinavia	1,330	430	260	820	2,840	4,740	3,790
United States	1,560	630	360	510	3,060	5,100	4,080
Average	1,800	410	210	580	3,000	5,000	4,000

Bread is very properly called the "staff of life," seeing that it supplies 60 per cent. of the sum total of energy in human food. Its consumption has increased prodigiously in recent years, owing to abundance and cheap prices. There has been a fall of 23 per cent. since the decade ending 1860 in the medium price for the world, that is to say, a man can now buy 100 lbs. of bread for what 77 would have cost in the years 1851–60, and as wages have risen 40 per cent. (see Chapter XX.), he can as easily buy 140 lbs. as he could then 77—a difference as regards the welfare of the masses that has not yet sufficiently attracted the notice of economists and philosophers.

The wheat-supply of the United Kingdom in the last forty-four years and consumption have been as follows:—

Years.	Million Bushels Consumed.			Price, Pence per Bushel.	Per Inhabitant.	
	British.	Imported.	Total.		Lbs. Wheat.	Cost, Shillings.
1841–60	103	33	136	81	273	32·8
1861–70	102	73	175	78	321	37·2
1871–80	77	114	191	72	325	34·8
1881–84	73	144	217	63	340	31·8

If our people had to pay now the average price that ruled from 1840 to 1860, the present consumption of wheat would cost 41 shillings per inhabitant, or 30 per cent. over the actual price.

Meat represents a greater cost than bread, although it stands for less than 10 per cent. of the total energy of food. In the United Kingdom we spend $2\frac{1}{2}$ times as much for meat as for bread. The following table shows the ratios of expenditure for the chief items of food:—

	U. Kingdom.	France.	Germany.	Russia.	Italy.	Europe.	U. States.
Grain	12	18	18	22	22	18	16
Meat	30	27	28	24	14	25	20
Liquor	21	22	20	17	21	20	14
Sundries	37	33	34	37	43	37	50
	100	100	100	100	100	100	100

The consumption of meat has always been considered a gauge of the comparative wealth of nations. In the words of Vauban, Bossuet, and Lagrange, "that country may be considered most prosperous in which the inhabitants are able to have the largest quantity of meat for their food," and in this respect France has made much advancement in our own days, as shown by the annual consumption, as follows:—

	Tons, 000's omitted.			Per Inhabitant, Lbs.		
	1840.	1860.	1880.	1840.	1860.	1880.
Beef	299	450	640	19	27	40
Mutton	82	114	210	5	7	12
Pork	290	378	305	19	23	19
Total	671	942	1,155	43	57	71

There can be no doubt that similar progress has taken place all over the European Continent, and that the consumption of meat is one-half more than it was in 1840–50. This, of course, is partly the result of the rapid increase of urban, and relative decline of rural, population. Dwellers in towns consume twice as much meat as those in the country, either because their work is more severe or their means are more affluent. In France, for example, 90 cities consume an aggregate quantity equal to 114 lbs. per inhabitant (the ratio for Paris being 187 lbs.), while the rest of the inhabitants have only 53 lbs. each.

In the United Kingdom the supply and consumption of meat have been as follows :—

Years.	Annual Slaughter, 000's omitted.			Consumption, 000's omitted.		Lbs. Per Inhab.
	Cattle.	Sheep.	Pigs.	Tons Meat.		
				Native.	Imported.	
1851-60	1,572	12,430	1,880	990	44	81
1861-70	1,790	13,672	2,043	1,106	131	91
1871-80	1,948	12,968	2,062	1,160	288	96
1881-83	1,996	12,440	2,080	1,195	447	105

In 1850 the consumption did not exceed 76 lbs., representing a value of 37 shillings; since then our population has risen 33 per cent., and the consumption per head 40 per cent.; so that, instead of 18,000 tons weekly, we now require nearly 32,000 tons, and as our flocks and herds can only supply 23,000, we have to import the remainder; in 1882 our people spent 80 shillings per head for meat, or more than twice as much as in 1850.

The Continent of Europe has apparently reached its maximum of meat production, and will henceforward be compelled either to import largely from other parts of the world or send away 3 million persons as emigrants yearly, unless the nations are disposed to reduce their consumption, which is not likely. The production of the Continent in 1882 was 7,190,000 tons, the consumption 7,270,000 tons, and this deficit of 80,000 tons was covered by imported meat from the United States.

The United States have a large surplus of meat, as shown by the quantities exported, viz. :—

	Tons, 000's omitted.			
	1861.	1871.	1881.	1884.
Bacon	22	32	336	173
Beef	6	20	68	87
Cattle	3	12	56	58
Pork	8	18	50	30
	89	82	510	348

At present the United States surplus may be estimated at 400,000 tons, but as the population of that country is increasing by 1½ million souls yearly, and likely to reach 88 millions by the close of the nineteenth century, there will be little if any available surplus ten years hence.

Australia and the River Plate republics must soon become the grazing-farms from which Europe (and especially Great Britain) will have to draw the meat-supply, which is now mainly derived from the United States. The actual deficit between England and the Continent is almost 12,000 tons *weekly*, which before the close of the century will probably reach 20,000 tons, or one million tons per annum. That is to say, Europe will require one-ninth of her supply, or equal to six weeks' consumption, from the southern hemisphere. The available surplus that may be obtained from there annually is shown thus:—

	Tons, 000's omitted.		
	River Plate.	Australia.	Total.
Beef	650	310	960
Mutton	520	450	970
Pork	11	24	35
Total	1,181	784	1,965

It is to be regretted that the people of the River Plate republics, instead of devoting their attention to so lucrative a business as supplying Europe with meat (more especially as the supply from the United States is declining), have gone into sugar-planting, domestic manufactures, flax-cultivation, and other industries of little profit to mankind at large, an insane system of "protective" duties at Buenos

Ayres and Montevideo enabling numbers of the inhabitants to prosecute useless industries, at a profit to those immediately engaged and an onerous result to the general public. Sooner or later we must get 10,000 tons of meat weekly from the River Plate.

The meat production of Europe and North America in 1882 was as follows:—

Tons, 000's omitted.

	Beef.	Mutton.	Pork.	Fowl, &c.	Total.
United Kingdom	666	346	145	38	1,195
Continent	3,954	1,425	1,561	260	7,190
United States	1,750	340	1,420	60	3,570
Canada	135	36	45	5	221
	6,505	2,137	3,171	363	12,176

The average annual consumption of meat is 60 lbs. per inhabitant on the Continent of Europe, 105 in United Kingdom, and 120 in United States, that of grain being much higher on the Continent than in this country or with the Americans. There is no better proof of the affluence of the people of the United Kingdom than the fact that they consume, per head, twice as much dairy products and four times as much sugar as the average among other nations.

The following table shows the annual consumption per inhabitant:—

	Lbs. per Inhabitant.					Gallons per Inhabitant.	
	Grain.	Meat.	Sugar.	Salt.	Butter, &c.	Liquor.	Equivalent in Alcohol.
Great Britain	340	105	72	40	26	30	1·92
France	405	74	21	30	7	26	2·65
Germany	415	69	21	25	12	24	1·60
Russia	440	48	7	19	6	3	1·05
Austria	390	64	14	14	8	15	1·45
Italy	320	23	7	18	3	18	1·76
Spain	360	49	5	17	2	14	1·48
Belgium and Holland	400	69	16	25	12	23	2·06
Scandinavia	370	67	24	25	16	12	2·40
United States	392	120	23	39	18	11	1·31
Average	405	70	20	32	11	16	1·50

Seeing the fall in wheat, it might be supposed that the cost of food to the working-classes and the world in general would be less now than thirty years ago, but such is not the case. The price-level has by no means moved in harmony with that of the rest of the world's products, as is apparent in the following table, which shows what the present quantities of food among nations would have cost at previous prices.

At Prices of	Food Value, Millions Sterling.	Ratio.	General Price-level.
1841–50	2,683	100	100
1851–60	3,046	113	105
1861–70	3,193	119	111
1871–80	3,208	120	106
1881–84	3,144	117	95

We find that the cost of food is now 17 per cent. higher than in 1841–50, although the total merchandise of the world shows a decline of 5 per cent.

Among the items (after meat) which have most contributed to the rise of the price-level of food are dairy products, and these enter so largely into the economy of human diet that they represent double the energy of meat, or about one-seventh of the total. The supply is unequal to the demand, and hence prices in Europe have risen 44 per cent. since the decade ending 1850. Not only Great Britain but the United States suffer such a deficit of eggs that they have to import large quantities. Since 1881 the average number imported into the United Kingdom is 20 millions *weekly*, or very close on one-third of the total consumption, and the United States receive 5 millions weekly from Denmark or Canada. Notwithstanding the invention of oleomargarine, Europe is unable to produce enough of butter and cheese, and imports 124,000 tons yearly, with ever-increasing requirements, since population is multiplying faster than cattle. There is, therefore, every likelihood of dairy products continuing to rise in value.

The consumption of wine and beer is on a vast scale, together making up 5500 million gallons, or 15 per inhabitant, the proportion being as 3 gallons of beer to 2 of wine. Excluding children, the consumption of wine and beer in Europe and United States is equal to 32 gallons per (adult) inhabitant, male and female. The production of wine has risen only 12 per cent. since 1850, having received such a check by the Phylloxera that 1½ million acres of vines have been pulled up in France since 1876. The price of common wines on the Continent has risen 48 per cent. since the decade ending 1850. The sum spent on beer, wine, spirits, cider, &c., in Europe is 10 per cent. more than on grain. In Great Britain it is almost double, although when all kinds of liquor are reduced to alcohol the ratio per inhabitant in this country is by no means high. This is the more remarkable seeing that drunkenness is such a fearful curse in the United Kingdom.

Sugar is now produced in such enormous quantities that the price is little more than half what it was thirty years ago, and some of the inferior kinds are said to be used as manure. The crop has quadrupled since 1850, that is, increased 10 times faster than population, the returns showing as follows:—

Year.	Tons, 000's omitted.		
	Cane.	Beetroot.	Total.
1851	978	162	1,140
1861	1,120	490	1,610
1871	1,700	1,400	3,100
1885	2,100	2,500	4,600

Tea, coffee, and tobacco are small items, together worth 95 millions sterling, or 3 per cent. of the total food expenditure. The production has been per annum as follows:—

	Tons.		Ratio.	
	1851–55.	1880–84.	1851–55.	1880–84.
Coffee	320,000	590,000	100	184
Tea	48,000	180,000	100	375
Tobacco	550,000	770,000	100	140

FOOD-SUPPLY.

The consumption of tobacco for smoking averages 44 oz. per inhabitant, against 40 oz. thirty years ago, in Europe; but there is also a large quantity now used for sheep-wash and other chemical purposes.

The principal facts in this chapter are these:—

First. That the money paid for food represents 45 per cent. of the earnings of all nations.

Secondly. That the surplus of earnings over cost of food is largest in Great Britain, United States, and France, and consequently the power of consumption of commodities.

Thirdly. That the average cost of food is 9 pence a day in Great Britain, 7 pence in United States, and 5 pence on the Continent, per inhabitant.

Fourthly. That the working-man in Europe can now buy 140 lbs. bread with the same amount of labour as 77 lbs. in the decade ending 1860.

Fifthly. That Great Britain drew one-fourth of her wheat-supply from abroad in the years 1841–60, and at present draws two-thirds.

Sixthly. That the consumption of meat per inhabitant has risen 40 per cent. in Great Britain and 42 per cent. on the Continent since 1850.

Seventhly. That Europe imports 600,000 tons of meat yearly from other parts of the globe, and that the United States will soon have no surplus for exportation, which will compel us to depend on Australia and the River Plate.

Eighthly. That dairy products have risen 44 per cent. since 1850 all over Europe, and that Great Britain derives 30 per cent. of her eggs and 50 per cent. of her butter and cheese from other nations.

XV.

POPULATION.

PRICES are often seriously affected or permanently altered by the increase or decrease of inhabitants. The value of land, the rent of houses, and many market-prices depend more or less on the density of population; for example, if Great Britain had now no more inhabitants than in 1850, the price of meat, butter, and eggs would be less. There is a normal law as regards population, whereby it increases about 1 per cent. per annum, unless checked by unhealthy agencies. The following table needs no explanation:—

	Millions.			Inhabitants per Square Mile.		
	1850.	1870.	1885.	1850.	1870.	1885.
England	17·9	22·7	27·5	310	390	465
Scotland	2·8	3·3	3·9	94	110	130
Ireland	6·6	5·5	4·9	205	170	155
United Kingdom	27·3	31·5	36·3	230	265	307
France	35·7	38·2	37·7	170	182	180
Germany	33·5	40·8	47·5	160	195	227
Russia	59·8	73·7	88·8	27	33	40
Austria	30·2	35·8	39·2	125	148	162
Italy	20·2	26·4	29·3	176	230	255
Spain	14·0	16·7	16·6	70	84	84
Portugal	3·4	3·8	4·4	100	110	130
Belgium	4·3	5·1	5·7	380	450	505
Holland	3·2	3·6	4·2	250	280	328
Denmark	1·4	1·8	2·1	100	120	133
Sweden	3·5	4·2	4·7	21	25	27
Norway	1·4	1·8	2·0	12	14	15
Switzerland	2·4	2·6	2·9	148	160	176
Greece	1·1	1·5	1·9	58	75	84
Servia	1·1	1·6	1·9	...	...	...
Roumania	4·0	4·8	5·4	...	...	...
Europe	246·5	293·9	330·6	70	80	90
United States	23·2	38·6	57·0	11	12	16
Canada	2·5	3·8	4·6	...	...	1
South America	24·1	25·2	27·0	3	3	3
Australia	0·9	1·8	3·3	...	...	1
Total	297·2	363·3	422·5	...	...	...

As a rule the richest nations are those which are most populous, for we find earnings low in such sparsely inhabited countries as Spain or Russia, and high in Great Britain and Belgium. Thus where hands are most abundant labour is not cheap—quite the reverse. Moreover, wages in England are higher to-day than when, thirty years ago, we had only 310 persons to the square mile, whereas now we have 465; that is to say, three persons stand where two stood before. Our population is twelve times as dense as that of Russia, and yet our working man earns two and a half times the Russian's wage.

If we take thirty-five years for a generation, we find that the mean increase of population in that interval is 42 per cent., as appears from the sum of the foregoing table. In Europe, however, collectively the increase has been only 35 per cent. (which is very much less than the normal rate of 1 per cent. per annum), owing to the tide of emigration. The percentages of increase in the various countries have been as follows:—

	Per Cent.		Per Cent.		Per Cent.
U. Kingdom	33	Portugal	30	Roumania	35
France	6	Belgium	33	Europe	35
Germany	42	Holland	31	United States	145
Russia	49	Denmark	50	Canada	84
Austria	30	Sweden	34	South America	12
Italy	46	Norway	44	Australia	266
Spain	18	Switzerland	21	Average	42

The most extraordinary movement of population in modern times has been the outflow of Europeans to the newer parts of the world, no fewer than 15 millions having emigrated since 1850, of whom 70 per cent. went to the United States. They were, for the most part, in the bloom of life, as may be concluded from the official reports in the United States, showing a natural increase of population (that is, excess of births over deaths) double the ordinary rate of Europe, viz.:—

98 HISTORY OF PRICES.

Ratio of Increase of Population in United States.

Period.	Natural.	Immigrants.	Total.
1851-60	24·2	11·4	35·6
1861-70	15·4	7·2	22·6
1871-80	22·8	7·3	30·1

One of the distinctive features of the last thirty years has been the relative decline of rural, and preponderance of urban, population. In England the twelve great towns, headed by London, represented 26 per cent. of the population in 1881, against 21 per cent. in 1841. In France nine cities held less than 5 per cent. (4·8) of the kingdom in 1835, and now hold 10½ per cent. In United States the urban population by the census of 1880 was 18¼ per cent., against 9 per cent. in 1840. Taking the term "urban population" to apply to all towns of 20,000 souls and upwards, we find the ratio in the different countries as follows:—

	Per Cent.		Per Cent.		Per Cent.
England	44	Austria	7	Sweden	8
Scotland	35	Italy	16	Norway	11
Ireland	19	Spain	12	Switzerland	8
United Kingdom	39	Portugal	10	Europe	15
France	18	Belgium	27	United States	18
Germany	16	Holland	28	Canada	9
Russia	6	Denmark	13	Australia	25

Increase of urban population is closely connected with manufactures and attended by a larger consumption of food and all commodities, and a better system of transport and distribution—circumstances that have direct influence on prices.

In considering the industrial power of nations it is essential to ascertain the proportion of bread-winners, in other words, to fix accurately the number of mouths depending for food on each able-bodied male, viz.:—

POPULATION.

Mouths to be fed by 100 Male Adults.

England . . 438	France . 387	United States . 440
Scotland . . 463	Germany . 417	Spain . . . 388
Ireland . . 476	Austria . 413	Holland & Belgium 404
United Kingdom 448	Italy . 424	Sweden . . 420

Thus the burthen on each male adult in Ireland is 10 per cent. heavier than in England, 22 per cent. more than in France.

The death-rate must also be noted, for it is certain that an unhealthy nation has never yet been a prosperous one. The following table shows the annual death-rate per 1000 inhabitants for various countries, and the loss of work by days of sickness, according to Farr's formula, to each male or female adult yearly :—

	Death-Rate.	Days of Sickness.		Death-Rate.	Days of Sickness.
Great Britain .	22	11	Italy . .	30	15
Ireland . .	18	9	Scandinavia .	20	10
France . .	24	12	Europe . .	30	15
Germany .	26	13	United States .	22	11
Austria . .	34	17	Australia . .	16	8

Sickness is a fearful tax in some countries, and is much increased, as in the case of Austria, by the unwise duties on salt, a commodity of foremost importance for health. Salt duties on the Continent vary from 4 pence to 28 pence per inhabitant, producing altogether 12 millions sterling per annum; if they cause 10 per cent. of the sickness, the loss in workmen's wages will be 18 millions sterling yearly.

The principal points that call for notice in this chapter are these :—

First. That the population of the civilised world was barely 300 millions in 1850, and is now 422 millions, having increased 42 per cent. in one generation.

Secondly. That the price of land depends mainly on population; Great Britain has twelve times the population of

Russia to the square mile, and land in this country is fifteen times as valuable as in the valley of the Don.

Thirdly. That rural population is declining in Europe, and that 11 millions of people have emigrated to the United States since 1850, mostly from rural districts, where hand labour has been displaced by machinery.

Fourthly. That in densely populated countries like Great Britain or Belgium wages are higher than in thinly peopled, like Spain or Russia.

Fifthly. That the number of able-bodied men is relatively highest in France and lowest in Ireland, and that the number of mouths to be fed by the labour of each male adult is 10 per cent. greater in Ireland than in England.

Sixthly. That the death-rate of Australia is only half that of Europe, and that the loss of labour from sickness is in some parts of Europe a heavy drawback.

Seventhly. That salt duties seriously affect public health, and seem to cause a greater loss in wages than the amount produced by the tax.

Eighthly. That the better health of our people enables us to work at greater advantage than most other nations.

XVI.

EMIGRATION AND COLONIES.

EMIGRATION from Europe received great impulse from the gold discoveries in California and Australia, 1849–51, and was destined subsequently to have unforeseen effects on the prices of two great staples. Gold-diggers in Australia became sheep-farmers, and German settlers in the Western States of America devoted themselves to grain-growing; in this manner the production of wool and wheat rose with a rapidity of which history affords no parallel.

In thirty-four years ending 1884 the emigration was as follows:—

	United States.	British Colonies.	South America.	Total.	Annual Average.
British [1]	4,655	2,120	82	6,857	202
Germans	4,020	170	72	4,262	125
Italians	222	14	742	978	29
Scandinavians	556	15	16	587	17
Spaniards	101	5	402	508	15
French	330	25	81	436	13
Swiss	140	12	64	216	6
Various	816	185	244	1,245	37
Total	10,840	2,546	1,703	15,089	444

Here we see a steady outflow of half a million souls per annum, three-fourths being of working age. The ratio among British and Germans was 60 males to 40 females, and among Spaniards and Italian 70 to 30. As regards con-

[1] Including 368,000 from Canada.

dition, only 10 per cent. of those who sailed from the Continent were cabin passengers, whereas in the United Kingdom there were 24 per cent.; and as cabin passengers are generally persons of more instruction, capital, and enterprise, we may consider the British (including Irish) emigrants were the best. British emigration is classified thus:—

Period.	000's omitted.				Destination, 000's omitted.			
	English.	Scotch.	Irish.	Total.	U. States.	Canada.	Australia.	Cape, &c.
1851-60	640	183	1,231	2,054	1,257	222	494	81
1861-70	650	158	867	1,675	1,185	136	272	82
1871-84	1,567	289	904	2,760	1,835	326	490	109
34 years	2,857	630	3,002	6,489	4,277	684	1,256	272

The bulk of the Irish went to the United States, from which country they remitted between 1851 and 1884 a sum exceeding 28 millions sterling to their distressed relatives at home.

According to the United States census of 1880, there were still surviving more than 60 per cent. of the Europeans who had landed there since 1820, viz. :—

	000's omitted.		Ratio of Survivors.
	Arrived.	Living in 1880.	
Germans	3,212	1,967	61·3
Irish	3,538	1,855	52·5
British	1,301	917	70·5
Scandinavians	427	376	88·1
French	345	107	31·0
Various	1,458	1,104	75·8
Total	10,281	6,326	61·3

The influx of settlers into the United States since 1850 has been :—

EMIGRATION AND COLONIES.

Period.	British.	Others.	Total.	Percentage of British.
	000's omitted			
1851-60	1,257	1,341	2,598	48
1861-70	1,185	1,308	2,493	48
1871-84	1,835	3,914	5,749	32
Thirty-four years	4,277	6,563	10,840	39

Emigration to America or Australia is likely to increase very much in the next ten years, not so much from over pressure of population as by reason of military service, and also because of the growing deficit of meat and dairy products. Every new adult settler in the United States, male or female, is valued as an increase of £160 to public wealth, which is exactly borne out in fact: the wealth of the United States between 1870 and 1880 rose 2420 millions sterling, or £53 per head, and as a colonist's life may be set down at thirty years, it follows that he adds £160 to the republic. Dr. Farr valued an English farm labourer as equal to an active capital of £246; Engel considers an adult male or female represents an amount of energy equal to £200; and in Australia every settler, big or little, is found to increase the revenue in the same degree as if £260 had been added to the public wealth.

We have seen that the British Colonies absorbed 2½ million settlers from 1850 to 1884, and of these no less than 84 per cent. were British. Excluding India, we find the growth of trade and population has been as follows:—

	Population, 000's omitted.			Commerce, Millions £.		
	1850.	1870.	1884.	1850.	1870.	1883.
Canada	2,470	3,810	4,560	6·7	34·8	51·4
Australia	480	1,820	3,220	10·5	57·3	115·3
South Africa	290	870	1,530	1·7	5·9	14·1
West Indies	860	1,230	1,420	8·4	14·5	19·7
Ceylon	1,640	2,260	2,650	3·8	8·4	7·9
Mauritius	170	330	368	4·2	4·2	6·6
Straits Settlement	260	290	315	6·5	18·7	37·6
Various	370	680	1,230	3·6	10·4	49·2
Total	6,540	11,290	15,293	45·4	154·2	301·8

The ratio of commerce to population is £20 per head, against £7 in 1850. The British Colonies, therefore, stand in a foremost rank for commercial activity, the ratio in Europe being only £7, in United States £5, per head. They are, moreover, the best customers for British manufactures, as shown thus:—

British Manufactures Consumed per Inhabitant.

Europe.	s.	America.	s.	British Colonies.	s.
France	16	United States	13	Australia	166
Germany	14	Mexico	4	Canada	42
Russia	2	Brazil	14	West Indies	56
Austria	1	River Plate	42	South Africa	67
Italy	6	Peru	5	Mauritius	32
Spain	6	Chili	14	Singapore	178
Average.	6	Average.	14	Average.	98

It is by no means surprising to find that the revenues and debt of the Colonies have grown with extraordinary rapidity, viz.:—

	Revenue, 000's omitted.			Debt, 000's omitted.		
	1850. £	1870. £	1884. £	1860. £	1870. £	1884. £
Australia	930	9,585	22,610	10,680	36,170	112,720
Canada	1,080	3,580	7,940	14,230	16,990	38,210
South Africa	515	958	6,065	420	1,375	23,365
West Indies	730	1,444	2,072	1,490	1,595	2,330
Various	1,320	2,510	3,630	215	2,050	3,405
Total	4,575	18,077	42,317	27,035	58,180	180,030

It is a striking proof of the elasticity and resources of the Colonies that Australia, for example, has a revenue of £7 per head, or three times as much as in Great Britain. The aggregate debt of 180 millions averages £15 per head, the ratio in Australia being £34; but the burthen is not felt as in Europe, partly because much of the revenue arises from public lands, and partly because of the wealth of the inhabitants.

EMIGRATION AND COLONIES.

Compare the public revenue, debt, and commerce of the Colonies with European states:—

	Per Inhabitant, Sterling.			Ratio of Debt to Revenue.
	Revenue.	Debt.	Commerce.	
Australia	7	34	35	486 to 100
Canada	2	9	11	450 „ 100
Cape Colony	5	19	12	380 „ 100
France	3	27	9	900 „ 100
Italy	2	16	3	800 „ 100
Great Britain	2½	20	19	800 „ 100
Russia	1	6	1½	600 „ 100
Spain	2	23	4	1,150 „ 100
Portugal	1½	21	3	1,400 „ 100

It appears, therefore, that the relative burthen of debt in our Colonies (averaging four and a half times revenue) is little more than half what it is in the principal countries of Europe.

The principal facts to be remembered are these:—

First. That 15 millions of people, or about 5 per cent. of the population of Europe, have emigrated since 1850—two-thirds to the United States—and that three-fourths of them were in the bloom of life, and about 90 per cent. of the peasant class.

Secondly. That but for the industry of these emigrants in North America and the southern hemisphere the prices of wheat and wool would be 30 or 40 per cent. higher than at present.

Thirdly. That new settlers add to the wealth, revenue, and commerce of a country, representing productive capital equal to £200 per head.

Fourthly. That the trade of the British Colonies has grown sevenfold since 1850, or three times faster than population.

Fifthly. That foreign countries consume British manufactures in this ratio; in Europe 6 shillings, in America 14 shillings, and in the British Colonies 98 shillings per inhabitant.

Sixthly. That the public debt in our Colonies averages $4\frac{1}{2}$ years of revenue, against 8 years in Great Britain and 9 years in France.

Seventhly. That emigration from Europe averages 500,000 persons yearly, and will probably reach a million by the close of the nineteenth century.

XVII.

WEALTH AND EARNINGS.

INDUSTRIES and prices depend in some manner on the wealth and earnings of a country. Rich nations will always be the largest consumers, and hence we see that Great Britain has the most extensive import trade in the world, while Spain and Russia occupy a low position in this respect. If we judge nations either by the accumulated wealth to population or by the average earnings per inhabitant, we find the order of priority as follows :—

Wealth.

1. United Kingdom.	6. United States.	11. Switzerland.
2. Holland.	7. Sweden.	12. Austria.
3. France.	8. Canada.	13. Spain.
4. Denmark.	9. Belgium.	14. Italy.
5. Australia.	10. Germany.	15. Russia.

Earnings.

1. Australia.	6. France.	11. Austria.
2. United Kingdom.	7. Denmark.	12. Switzerland.
3. United States.	8. Belgium.	13. Spain.
4. Canada.	9. Germany.	14. Italy.
5. Holland.	10. Sweden.	15. Russia.

In 1880 the wealth of twenty principal nations summed up 50,750 millions sterling, under eight items, viz. :—

	Millions £.	Percentage.
Lands	16,939	33·4
Houses	12,206	24·1
Public works	7,264	14·3
Furniture	6,098	12·0
Cattle	2,101	4·1
Merchandise	1,292	2·5
Bullion	957	1·9
Sundries	3,893	7·7
Total	50,750	100·0

Land is by far the foremost element of public wealth, and yet nothing is more uncertain in price; poor land in the settled parts of Canada is worth £8 an acre, while the rich pampas of the Argentine Republic may be bought at 15 shillings. Farms of superior fertility in Russia are sold at £5 an acre, which would sell at £40 in England, and at £60 in France, Belgium, or Denmark. It is not quality that determines the value of land, but accidental circumstances, such as facilities for sending products to market, security for life and property, and often the character of the laws and people. Land in New Zealand carrying one sheep to the acre averages £5, but the estancias of Buenos Ayres carrying four sheep per acre may be had, some distance inland, at 10 shillings an acre. The following table shows the price of land in different countries:—

£ Sterling per Acre.					
U. Kingdom	33	Austria	15	Belgium	48
France	36	Italy	22	Holland	42
Germany	25	Spain	18	Denmark	33
Russia	3	Portugal	25	Sweden	12

Small ownership, as in France, gives an enhanced value, the assessments in that country for 1875 ranging from £48 to £66 per acre for good land; the number of holders averaging ten acres being no fewer than $2\frac{1}{2}$ millions, or three-fourths of the total.

WEALTH AND EARNINGS.

Houses constitute one-fourth of the wealth of mankind, and vary from £11 per inhabitant in Russia to £65 in Great Britain. The money expended yearly in building ranges from 8 to 40 shillings per inhabitant, as regards countries, but is much higher in cities, the average in recent years being as follows:—

Shillings per Inhabitant.

New York	.	88	Buenos Ayres	61	Glasgow	.	52
London	.	77	Liverpool	. 59	Monte Video		39
Toronto	.	69	Paris .	. 55	Turin .	.	22

In Great Britain the value of house property has grown much faster than population, the average per house having risen 75 per cent. since 1851, viz.:—

Year.	Houses, 000's omitted.	Rental, Millions £.	Rental, £ per House.	Rental, £ Per Inhabitant.
1851	3,648	44·3	12·1	2·2
1861	4,139	58·2	14·0	2·5
1871	4,672	74·5	16·0	2·9
1881	5,475	114·2	21·0	3·8

The house property of the United Kingdom shows the following averages to population:—£12 in Ireland, £60 in Scotland, £66 in the provinces of England, and £158 in London, per inhabitant.

Public works in 1880 included 4005 millions sterling for railways, the rest being made up of roads, bridges, canals, drainage, harbours, &c. The value of public works, not railways, is less than £4 per inhabitant in Spain, and over £15 in France or Great Britain. The following table shows the wealth of the principal countries:—

HISTORY OF PRICES.

	Millions Sterling.					Ratio per Inhabitant. £
	Agricultural.	Urban.	Public Works.	Sundries.	Total.	
United Kingdom	2,210	3,675	1,317	1,518	8,720	249
France	3,060	3,082	1,084	834	8,060	218
Germany	2,526	2,485	909	403	6,323	140
Russia	2,095	1,570	533	145	4,343	53
Austria	1,711	1,303	443	156	3,613	95
Italy	963	1,030	239	119	2,351	82
Spain	779	550	139	125	1,593	93
Portugal	195	113	27	36	371	88
Belgium	331	237	102	136	806	145
Holland	330	158	352	147	987	240
Denmark	269	54	21	22	366	198
Sweden	384	209	58	44	695	152
Norway	141	96	19	26	282	147
Greece	125	63	7	16	211	125
Switzerland	140	106	63	15	324	118
Europe	15,259	14,731	5,313	3,742	39,045	123
United States	2,961	3,887	1,717	930	9,495	190
Canada	259	234	102	55	650	148
Mexico	173	364	24	77	638	90
Argentine Republic	208	88	22	14	332	130
Australia	318	154	86	32	590	197
The World	19,178	19,458	7,264	4,850	50,750	133

Three countries, namely, Great Britain, United States, and France, represent one-half the total wealth of nations, and the accumulations of these countries since 1850 will be seen in the following statement:—

	Wealth, Millions Sterling.			£ per Inhabitant.		
	1850.	1870.	1880.	1850.	1870.	1880.
United Kingdom	5,160	6,880	8,410	190	220	242
France	3,170	5,240	8,060	89	133	218
United States	1,686	7,074	9,495	75	185	190
Total	9,801	19,194	25,965	114	176	208

In the whole term of thirty years France accumulated 163 millions, the United States 260 millions, and the United Kingdom 110 millions sterling per annum, that is, an aggregate of 533 millions yearly, being equal to an average of

3 pence per inhabitant daily in the United Kingdom, 3½ pence in France, and almost 3 pence (2·8) in the United States for the medium population in the said period.

Although the United Kingdom is the richest nation in the world, with reference to population, there is excessive disparity between the British (properly so-called) and their Irish fellow-subjects, as appears from the legacy, income-tax, and other returns. The following table shows the wealth of the three kingdoms in 1801 and in 1882 :—

	\multicolumn{6}{c}{Millions Sterling.}
	England.		Scotland.		Ireland.	
	1801.	1882.	1801.	1882.	1801.	1882.
Lands	718	1,403	102	207	170	270
Houses	240	2,007	30	213	36	60
Sundries	566	3,768	78	570	90	222
Total	1,524	7,178	210	990	296	552

The percentages of the three kingdoms in 1801 were, England 75, Ireland 15, and Scotland 10; but at present Ireland hardly exceeds 6 per cent., as appears from the following statement :—

	\multicolumn{4}{c}{Distribution of Wealth, Percentage.}
	Legacy Tables of 1877.	Income-Tax of 1880.	Dictionary of Statistics.	General Average.
England	82·3	84·2	82·3	82·9
Scotland	12·2	9·6	11·4	11·1
Ireland	5·5	6·2	6·3	6·0
Total	100·0	100·0	100·0	100·0

The ratio of wealth in Ireland is only £110 per inhabitant, against £260 in Scotland and £276 in England; as a consequence the incidence of taxation in Ireland is twice as heavy as in Great Britain. In wealth to population Ireland is not so poor as Italy or Spain, but is considerably below Sweden, Germany, or Switzerland.

The earnings of nations can only be ascertained from the value of food and other merchandise which they consume and the increase of accumulated wealth in a given number of years. Hence the income of a whole people cannot be gauged with the same precision as the amount of capital or wealth which they possess, but the following table may be relied upon for 1880 as being within 5 per cent. of the reality :—

	Popular Earnings, Millions Sterling.			£ per Inhabitant per Annum.
	Agricultural.	Various.	Total.	
United Kingdom	263	984	1,247	35·2
France	435	530	965	25·7
Germany	444	406	850	18·7
Russia	482	366	848	10·1
Austria	307	295	602	16·3
Italy	174	171	345	11·5
Spain	133	85	218	13·0
Portugal	30	31	61	14·0
Belgium	44	76	120	22·1
Holland	45	59	104	26·0
Denmark	37	10	47	23·2
Sweden	41	39	80	18·0
Norway	14	10	24	13·0
Switzerland	18	26	44	16·0
Greece	9	14	23	11·8
Europe	2,476	3,102	5,578	18·0
United States	544	876	1,420	27·2
Canada	52	66	118	26·9
Australia	76	57	133	43·4
Argentine Republic	34	27	61	23·3
Total	3,182	4,128	7,310	19·5

It appears that 44 per cent. of the earnings of mankind are agricultural; but in the United Kingdom the ratio does not exceed 21, and even in the United States it is but 38 per cent. On the other hand, in Russia it is 57, in Spain 60, per cent., both of which countries are very poor. It is only by the use of improved machinery that agriculture can now be carried on with profit, and in this respect Russia and Spain are still very backward.

WEALTH AND EARNINGS.

The following table shows the cost of living in the principal countries and the daily expenditure per inhabitant:—

	Millions Sterling.				Pence Daily per Inhabitant.			
	Food.	Clothing.	Sundries.	Total.	Food.	Clothing.	Sundries.	Total.
United Kingdom	473	138	482	1,093	9·0	2·6	9·2	20·8
France	387	112	321	820	7·0	2·2	6·2	15·4
Germany	440	110	244	794	7·0	1·8	4·0	12·8
Russia	511	122	157	790	4·1	1·1	1·4	6·6
Austria	320	90	152	562	5·8	1·6	2·7	10·1
Italy	186	50	76	312	4·4	1·2	1·8	7·4
Spain & Portugal	152	36	71	259	4·8	1·2	2·4	8·4
Belgium & Holland	100	30	74	204	6·7	2·1	5·0	13·8
Scandinavia	74	21	44	139	6·0	1·6	3·5	11·1
Europe	2,643	709	1,621	4,973	6·0	1·6	3·6	11·2
United States	534	240	436	1,210	7·0	3·1	5·5	15·6
Total	3,177	949	2,0579	6,183	6·1	1·9	4·1	12·1

The average cost of living for all nations is one shilling daily per inhabitant, *i.e.*, 20 pence for a man, 16 for a woman, and 8 for a child.

The distribution of the year of 300 working-days in various countries is as follows:—

		Days devoted to Pay for			
	Food.	Clothing.	House Rent.	Taxes.	Sundries.	Total.
Great Britain	114	34	29	32	91	300
France	120	36	30	45	69	300
Germany	155	40	27	38	40	300
Italy	162	44	24	60	10	300
Belgium	133	40	20	33	74	300
Russia	180	49	20	37	14	300
Austria	159	43	22	34	42	300
Spain	164	41	24	56	15	300
Scandinavia	147	40	23	30	60	300
Europe	140	40	27	40	53	300
United States	113	49	30	33	75	300

Sundries include savings, which stand for 36 days in Great Britain, 50 in France, and 43 in United States.

The principal facts to be remembered are:—

H

First. That the aggregate wealth of twenty principal nations amounts to 51,000 millions sterling, and their annual earnings to 7,300 millions.

Secondly. That lands, cattle, and farming implements make up 40 per cent. of the total wealth, and that agricultural earnings average $16\frac{1}{2}$ per cent. on capital.

Thirdly. That the value of land is for the most part accidental, depending less on fertility than on the number of inhabitants and the liberty and security which they enjoy.

Fourthly. That houses represent one-fourth of the wealth of mankind, and that house rent takes the labour of 27 days of each year in Europe and 30 in United States.

Fifthly. That the average of wealth to population is highest in the United Kingdom, and of earnings highest in Australia.

Sixthly. That accumulations or savings average 3 pence daily per inhabitant in the United Kingdom, $3\frac{1}{2}$ pence in France, and $2\frac{3}{4}$ pence in the United States.

Seventhly. That the total expenditure of nations averages 6 pence daily per inhabitant for food, 2 pence for clothing, and 4 pence for rent, taxes, and sundries; in all, a shilling (12·1) per day.

Eighthly. That after paying for food, clothing, rent, and taxes, an Englishman has 91 days of the year for leisure or luxuries, an American 75, a Frenchman 69, a German 40, a Russian 14, an Italian 10.

Ninthly. That the relative wealth, or surplus for leisure, determines not only house rent but the prices of many articles of luxury in the various countries.

XVIII.

SUMMARY OF INDUSTRIES.

THE principal countries of Europe, combined with the United States, make up a total of 88 millions able-bodied men, of whom a little more than half are engaged in agriculture. The following table shows them under seven classes of occupation:—

Adult Males, 000's omitted.

	Agriculture.	Seamen.	Railways.	Manufacturers.	Miners.	Army and Navy.	Various.	Total.
U. Kingdom	1,120	360	262	1,562	538	249	3,625	7,716
France	5,045	129	234	1,660	206	580	2,038	9,892
Germany	4,746	67	301	2,555	231	466	2,768	11,134
Russia	17,038	97	160	610	207	870	2,030	21,012
Austria	5,220	16	125	816	92	301	2,915	9,485
Italy	5,044	126	61	319	32	690	934	7,206
Spain & Port.	1,823	76	62	385	85	186	2,780	5,397
Belg. & Holl.	1,110	34	56	440	110	120	548	2,418
Scandinavia	1,264	234	55	130	31	106	264	2,084
Europe	42,410	1,139	1,316	8,477	1,532	3,568	17,902	76,344
U. States	3,033	174	463	2,739	560	36	4,601	11,606
Total	45,443	1,313	1,779	11,216	2,092	3,604	22,503	87,950

In the above table "seamen" also include fishermen. The numbers engaged in manufactures can only be given approximately, as some countries include bakers and small tradesmen under this heading, while others count merely the operatives in factories or establishments employing over twenty hands.

Prices of grain, meat, &c., are invariably lower in countries where the bulk of the people are engaged in agriculture than in those which are given chiefly to manufactures. On the other hand, all manufactured products are cheaper in countries where agriculture is of little importance. The following table shows the ratio of industry :—

Occupation.	U. Kingdom.	France.	Germany.	Russia.	Europe.	U. States.
Agriculture	14·5	51·0	42·7	80·8	55·5	26·1
Seamen	4·7	1·3	0·6	0·5	1·5	1·5
Railways	3·4	2·4	2·7	0·8	1·8	4·0
Manufactures	20·2	16·8	23·0	2·9	11·1	23·6
Mines	7·0	2·1	2·1	1·0	2·0	4·8
Army and Navy	3·2	5·9	4·2	4·1	4·7	0·3
Various	47·0	20·5	24·7	9·9	23·4	39·7
Total	100·0	100·0	100·0	100·0	100·0	100·0

XIX.

GENERAL SURVEY OF PRICES.

BEFORE considering the rise or fall of price in the several items, it is expedient to sum up the value of the chief products of human industry according to the average of the years 1881–84 :—

	Millions Sterling.	Percentage.
Grain	1,326	25·3
Meat	830	15·8
Iron and steel wares	384	7·3
Dairy products	340	6·5
Cotton goods	302	5·7
Timber	273	5·2
Woollen goods	223	4·2
Beer	214	4·1
Coal	189	3·6
Leather	184	3·5
Potatoes	181	3·3
Wine	130	2·5
Spirits	128	2·5
Raw cotton	87	1·7
Wool	83	1·6
Books and journals	79	1·5
Silks	73	1·4
Linens, jute, &c.	70	1·3
Sugar	61	1·2
Coffee	42	0·8
Tobacco	37	0·7
Tea	16	0·3
Total	5,252	100·0

Here we see at a glance the relative importance of the several industries: grain, for example, is equal to the aggregate of the last 14 items, and meat is six times as important as wine or spirits. A rise or fall in wool or sugar would have trifling effect compared to one in grain, although an uninformed person would think the three items of nearly equal magnitude.

The wheat crop of the world in the years 1881–84 averaged 520 millions sterling, or 40 per cent. of all the grain. We have, moreover, evidence that the other kinds of grain generally rose or fell in sympathy with it, and hence I may be permitted to assume that variations in wheat have been common to all grain. The fluctuations in the price of wheat have been as follows:—

Years.	Pence per Bushel.			
	Great Britain.	Continent.	United States.	Medium.
1841–50	80	53	58	64
1851–60	82	72	79	78
1861–70	78	73	75	75
1871–80	71	74	65	70
1881–84	63	70	48	60

Taking the medium price, we find a fall of 23 per cent. since the decade ending 1860, but only of 6 per cent. as compared with 1841–50.

Meat, on the other hand, has risen, as appears from the prices in London and New York, viz.:—

Years.	Beef, £ Sterling per Ton.			
	London.	New York.	Medium.	Ratio.
1841–50	56	24	40	100
1851–60	61	28	45	112
1861–70	65	29	47	118
1871–80	79	27	53	133
1881–84	84	34	59	148

Here is a rise of 48 per cent. since 1850 in a commodity which constitutes one-sixth of the value represented by the world's products. In other words, the same quantity of meat for which nations now pay 830 millions sterling would have cost only 560 millions before the year 1850.

Iron and steel wares come next in importance, showing a heavy fall, thanks to the discoveries of science. The prices of pig iron in Great Britain and United States have been as follows :—

	Shillings per Ton.		
Years.	Great Britain.	United States.	Medium.
1841–50	68	134	101
1851–60	66	122	94
1861–70	59	123	91
1871–80	74	132	103
1881–84	52	98	75

This fall of 26 per cent. in the raw material is much less than has taken place in manufactured goods. Steel has come down 70 per cent. since the inventions of Bessemer and Siemens, that is, from £34 to £11 per ton. The average decline is 33 per cent., that is to say, 40 shillings will now buy as much hardware as 60 shillings would have done in 1841–50; a saving of 192 millions sterling per annum.

Cotton goods may be judged by English prices, this country being the chief seat of the industry, and it is very remarkable that while raw cotton has risen 15 per cent. the price of calico has fallen 22 per cent., which is doubtless explained by improved machinery. The prices have been :—

Years.	Cotton. Pence per Lb.	Calico. Pence per Yard.	Ratio.	
			Raw Cotton.	Calico.
1841–50	5·3	3·40	100	100
1851–60	5·9	2·90	111	85
1861–70	12·8	4·20	242	124
1871–80	7·1	3·00	133	88
1881–84	6·1	2·65	115	78

The cotton manufactures of all nations sum up a total of 302 millions sterling; the fall in price is therefore equivalent to 90 millions.

Wool and woollen goods have fallen very unequally, the former 43, the latter only 9 per cent. since 1860, viz. :—

Years.	Wool Pence per Lb.	Manufactures, Pence per Yd.		Ratio.	
		Carpets.	Flannel.	Wool.	Manufactures.
1851–60	21	32	16	100	100
1861–70	18	35	19	86	114
1871–80	14	34	18	67	109
1881–84	12	28	15	57	91

The fall in wool is mainly owing to the great increase of Colonial, which now forms 45 per cent. of the world's clip, against 10 per cent. in 1850.

Timber has fallen very heavily, from 80 shillings in the decade ending 1850 to 51 shillings per load in 1881–84.

Dairy products have risen, owing to the increased consumption per inhabitant all over Europe, the prices being as follows :—

Years.	Butter, per Cwt.		Cheese, per Cwt.		Eggs of 4 Nations per Doz.	Ratio.		
	England.	U.S.	England.	U.S.		Butter.	Cheese.	Eggs.
	s.	s.	s.	s.	d.			
1841–50	81	61	48	30	5·2	100	100	100
1851–60	82	90	50	39	5·7	121	114	110
1861–70	104	106	56	47	6·3	148	131	121
1871–80	110	104	56	52	7·6	151	138	146
1881–84	102	98	55	52	8·1	141	137	155

There is, on the whole, a rise of 44 per cent.; that is, men pay now 340 millions for what would have cost 236 millions in 1841–50.

Coal has varied less than most other things, the supply keeping pace pretty evenly with the demand: prices in Europe and America have been as follows :—

Years.	Shillings per Ton.			
	Gt. Britain.	Continent.	U.S.	Medium.
1841–50	8	10	21	13
1851–60	9	11	22	14
1861–70	10	12	20	14
1871–80	12	14	15	14
1881–84	9	11	12	11

In this item we have a saving of 33 millions sterling as compared with the prices of 1841-50.

Potatoes represent another industry of considerable magnitude, and one in which prices have risen beyond all expectation, viz.—

Years.	Shillings per Ton.			Ratio.
	Gt. Britain.	France.	Medium.	
1841-50	80	72	76	100
1851-60	84	80	82	108
1861-70	106	98	102	134
1871-80	110	105	108	142
1881-84	122	116	119	157

This rise of 57 per cent. is the more remarkable, as grain has fallen in the same period. Men pay 181 millions sterling for the same quantity of potatoes that would have cost 115 millions before 1850.

Wine has risen owing to the ravages of the phylloxera, the prices of the commonest kinds having been as follows :—

Years.	Pence per Gallon.			
	France.	Spain.	Italy.	Medium.
1841-50	18	12	13	14
1851-60	22	15	14	17
1861-70	23	16	15	18
1871-80	21	18	15	18
1881-84	27	19	16	21

Colonial products, namely, sugar, coffee, tea, and tobacco, have had very opposite fortunes, viz. :—

Years.	Shillings per Cwt.				Ratio.			
	Tea.	Coffee.	Sugar.	Tobacco.	Tea.	Coffee.	Sugar.	Tobacco.
1841-50	112	38	33	56	100	100	100	100
1851-60	140	51	31	86	125	134	94	154
1861-70	168	64	33	104	150	168	100	186
1871-80	150	88	26	73	133	230	79	130
1881-84	112	72	19	72	100	190	58	128

Taking these four products together there is apparently a medium rise of 19 per cent., but this is untrue, and shows how deceptive index numbers may prove. The same quantity of tea, coffee, sugar, and tobacco which cost 156 millions sterling in 1881–84 would have cost 172 millions before 1850. Therefore, instead of a rise, there has been on the whole a fall of 10 per cent.

The same quantities of products and merchandise consumed annually from 1881 to 1884 would have cost in previous periods, at the prices then ruling, as follows:—

	Millions Sterling.				
	1841–50.	1851–60.	1861–70.	1871–80.	1881–84.
Grain	1,419	1,724	1,658	1,547	1,326
Meat	560	628	661	747	830
Hardware	576	525	504	593	384
Dairy products	236	266	303	333	340
Cotton goods	386	335	484	346	302
Woollen goods	263	245	280	268	223
Timber	428	338	338	301	273
Coal	224	241	241	241	189
Leather	218	202	212	188	184
Potatoes	115	125	154	164	181
Wine	86	105	111	111	130
Raw cotton	76	85	183	101	87
Wool	160	145	125	97	83
Books	120	115	105	87	79
Silks	68	82	104	88	73
Linens, &c.	77	74	78	74	70
Sugar	106	100	106	84	61
Coffee	23	30	38	50	42
Tobacco	29	44	53	38	37
Tea	16	20	24	21	16
Total	5,186	5,429	5,762	5,479	4,910

The above twenty items comprise 90 per cent. of all human industries, as regards products or manufactures, and therefore enable us to arrive at the exact variations of price-level for the whole world, that is, the rise or fall in the purchasing power of gold since 1850. The result is as follows:—

Years.	
1841–50	100·0
1851–60	104·7
1861–70	111·1
1871–80	105·7
1881–84	94·7

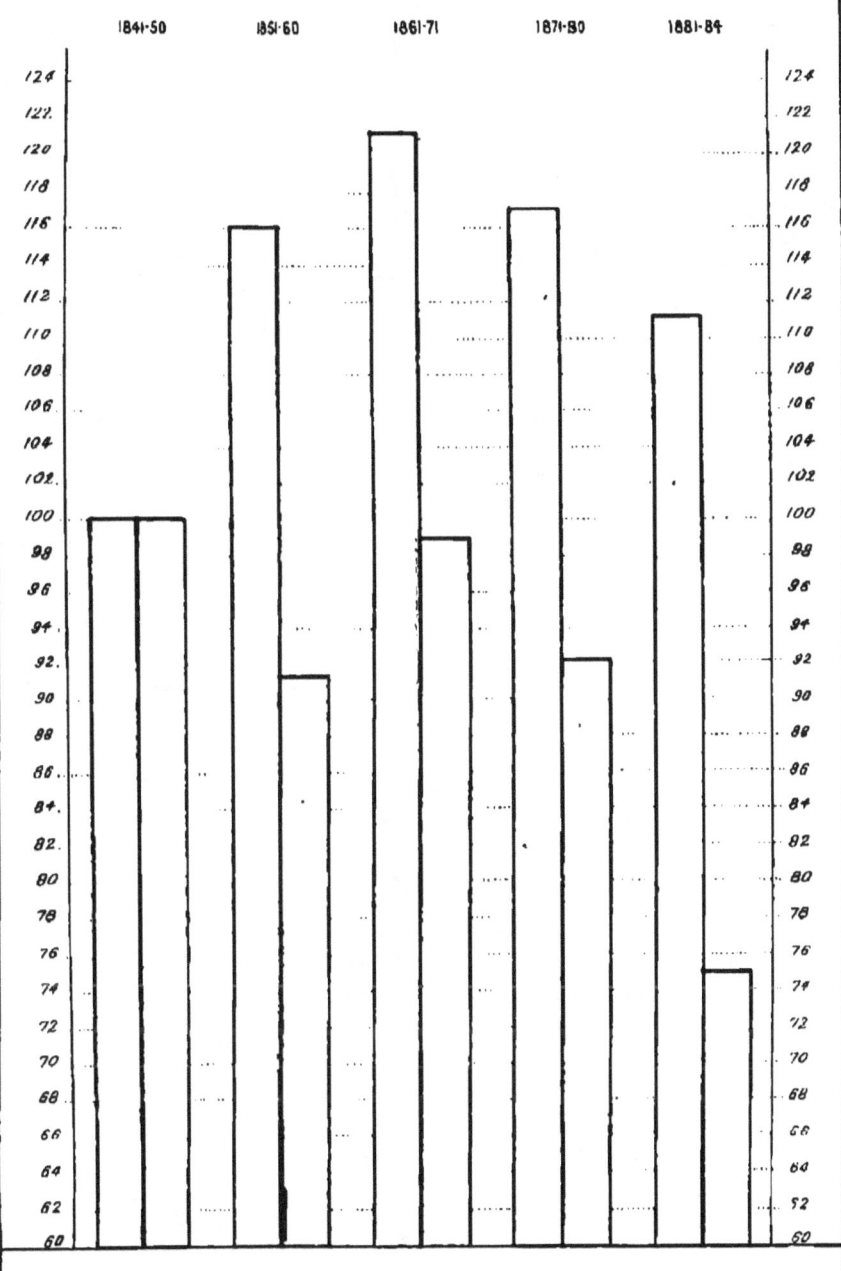

GENERAL SURVEY OF PRICES.

We find, therefore, a fall of $5\frac{1}{4}$ per cent. from the price-level of the decade ending 1850, or nearly 15 per cent. from that of 1861–70. This is much less than people in England generally suppose, because it is the fault of Englishmen to limit their scope of observation to this island, when, by looking around at other nations, we might be better disposed to form a correct judgment.

It is remarkable that if we separate agricultural (including pastoral) products from manufactures, we find the former have risen 11 per cent., the latter fallen 25 per cent., since 1850. The present volume of the world's products at previous prices would have represented the following values:—

Years.	Millions, £.		Ratio.	
	Agriculture.	Manufactures.	Agriculture.	Manufactures.
1841–50	2,826	2,360	100	100
1851–60	3,272	2,157	116	91
1861–70	3,416	2,346	121	99
1871–80	3,293	2,186	117	92
1881–84	3,133	1,777	111	75

Therefore, 15 shillings will now buy as much manufactures as 20 in the years 1841–50, but in matters of food we should require 22.

As regards the causes which led to the fall in price-level the reader is referred to Chapter XXII.

XX.

WAGES.

In Tooke and Newmarch's "History of Prices" (1785-1856) it is clearly proved that wages and prices do not always move together, but that one may rise when the other falls. Nevertheless, as wages enter largely into the cost of production, they must ultimately in some degree affect prices. The subject, however, is too large to be treated here in the manner it deserves, and would raise so many side issues that we should lose sight of the question before us.

As a matter of fact, wages have been rising in all countries in the last thirty years, and yet, as we have just seen, the price-level of the world has fallen 10 per cent. In like manner English operatives earn higher wages than those of any country in Continental Europe, which does not prevent us from producing cotton goods and other things much cheaper than any other country. Compare for a moment the cotton and woollen goods manufactured in Spain, at enormous prices, with those of England, and the wages earned by operatives in that country with ours: the contrast is astounding. If cheapness of labour meant cheapness of production, Ireland would possess such an advantage over England that this country would be unable to compete with her, and she would become a great manufacturing country. The same may be said of Italy.

Wages of all descriptions have risen about 40 per cent. since 1850, which some ascribe to the effect of the gold discoveries in California and Australia, others to the spread of public instruction, others to the greater efficiency of industry and demand for labour. But it seems more probably the result of railways and facilities for emigration, which enable the peasantry or artisans of one country to remove to another in quest of the highest reward for their work.

In the first place, as regards agricultural labour, we have only to compare the wages now general in various countries with the Parliamentary Report of 1835, containing minute returns by the British Secretaries of Legation in every part of Europe upon the wages then paid in the several kingdoms, viz. :—

Wages of Day Labourer.

	Pence.			Pence.	
	1835.	1884.		1835.	1884.
United Kingdom	16	28	Austria	10	20
France	15	25	Italy	5	12
Germany	8	18	Belgium & Holland	9	20
Russia	6	12	Scandinavia	8	14

We find that the medium in 1835 was 9½ pence, and in 1884 it was 18½ pence, having almost doubled. This is relatively a much greater increase than we find among artisans and other classes of skilled labour. Such has been the attraction that towns have had for the rural population that the peasantry who remained have been able to earn much higher wages than before.

The rise in artisans' wages in England and France is shown in the following table :—

	Pence per Day.					Medium Rise since 1840–50.
	England.			France.		
	1840.	1860.	1884.	1850.	1880.	
Blacksmith	42	56	64	25	35	45 per cent.
Mason	46	60	70	22	35	55 ,,
Carpenter	40	50	60	22	35	55 ,,
Plumber	44	60	70	22	33	55 ,,
Cotton-spinner	36	40	48	24	36	42 ,,

As compared, therefore, with 1850 we find a rise of 40 or 50 per cent., which is the more striking because the price of food (except meat, butter, and wine) has fallen in the interval. This fact suffices to explain the great development of savings-banks all over Europe, since a similar rise in wages has occurred in all countries.

According to the Census Reports of the United States, the average earnings of operatives since 1850 appear as follows :—

	£ per Annum.					
Years.	New England.	Middle States.	South.	West.	Average.	Pence Daily.
1850	51	51	40	58	51	40
1860	56	58	57	68	61	48
1870	73	72	43	64	69	53
1880	75	76	48	70	73	57

Here there is an increase of 44 per cent., showing that the wages of operatives have risen in the same degree both in Europe and in America. Meantime labour is more remunerative in the United States, because the surplus of earnings over the cost of food is much greater than in Europe; and the same may be said of Australia, as appears from the following table of wages and food :—

	Shillings per Week.			Percentage.	
	Wages.	Food.	Surplus.	Food.	Surplus.
Great Britain	31	14	17	45	55
France	21	12	9	57	43
Germany	16	10	6	62	38
Belgium	20	12	8	60	40
Italy	15	9	6	60	40
Spain	16	10	6	62	38
Europe	20	11	9	55	45
United States	48	16	32	33	67
Australia	40	12	28	30	70

The condition of the working-classes can only be considered satisfactory when a day's wages are more than the cost of two days' food, as happens in Great Britain, United

States, and Australia. It is significant of improvement that the profits earned by capital are much less than in past years, while the wages of labour are higher. In fact, so far from capitalists defrauding workmen of their fair wages, it is manifest that in Europe, and especially in England, the share of profit accruing to the employer of labour has almost reached a minimum, and that manufacturing industry will not be worth carrying on if his share be further diminished. The only real drawback that labour suffers is from the extravagant house rent that artisans have to pay in large towns, and for which municipal legislation ought and must provide a remedy.

In France, Germany, and other countries where money commands higher interest than in England (see page 19) the profits of the capitalist are larger, or else nobody would care to embark in industrial enterprises; thus if a millowner in Lancashire is content to earn 5 per cent., a similar employer in France or Germany must get 6 per cent., although his workmen earn less wages than with us. In a word, the competition of capital in the United Kingdom outweighs that of labour, whereas the reverse happens in most other countries. British operatives, as a rule, earn in wages from 30 to 33 per cent. of the value of the manufactures which they produce, but in the United States the workman gets only 18 per cent., although in other respects he is better off than his English brother. The relative share that labour earns in the United States is declining, as we see from the census returns, but it must be remembered that machinery plays such a transcendental part in America that we must always expect labour to form apparently a small ratio.

The following table from Census Reports shows the amount paid to operatives and the value of manufactures produced in the United States since 1850 :—

Year.	Millions Sterling.		Percentage of Wages.
	Wages.	Product.	
1850	49	211	23·3
1860	80	377	21·2
1870	161	846	19·0
1880	198	1,112	17·8

This small ratio of wages explains how Americans are able to compete with European nations where labour is cheaper, and to undersell even British manufacturers in many things.

American labour is much more productive than that of any other country, for three reasons : firstly, because the ratio of able-bodied men among the operatives is larger ; secondly, because machinery is brought to greater perfection and more universally used than in Europe ; thirdly, because " protective " duties give an artificial value to those products intended for home consumption. The average product of each operative in the various countries is :—

	£ per Annum.
Great Britain	185
France	179
Germany	111
Austria	112
United States	403

The product per operative in the United States has risen 83 per cent. since 1850, while wages have risen only 43 per cent., as seen in the following table :—

Wages and Product per Operative in £ Sterling.

States.	Wages.		Product.		Increase per Cent.	
	1850.	1880.	1850.	1880.	Wages.	Product.
New England	51	75	190	360	47	89
Middle	51	76	230	420	49	83
South	40	48	192	310	20	61
West	58	70	275	490	21	78
Average	51	73	220	403	43	83

Thus the improvement in production has been double the rise in wages, confirming the principle that the best-paid operatives are the most productive and consequently the cheapest.

The principal points in this chapter are :—

First. That wages often rise when prices fall, and *vice versâ*, as shown in many cases by Tooke and Newmarch.

Secondly. That since 1850 wages in Europe have risen very notably and prices fallen 5 per cent.

Thirdly. That English operatives are the best paid in Europe, and their work, after all, the cheapest.

Fourthly. That agricultural wages have risen 90 per cent., while those of artisans and mechanics only 50 per cent., since 1850.

Fifthly. That wages in Europe average 30 per cent., in United States 18 per cent., of the value of manufactured goods.

Sixthly. That American operatives have to pay only 33 per cent. of their earnings for food, while the average is 45 per cent. in Great Britain and 55 per cent. on the Continent.

Seventhly. That the share of the capitalist or employer is regulated by the ordinary rates of discount, and that he receives less in England, where money is cheap, than on the Continent.

Eighthly. That the average product per operative is highest in the United States, but that the nominal product is an artificial value caused by "protective" duties; nevertheless, after deducting for the inflation, his product is the highest.

XXI.

PRICES AND WAGES SINCE 1782.

Although the scope of the present work goes back no further than the year 1850, it may be to the purpose to take a glance at the prices and wages of the last hundred years. In the first place, as regards Great Britain, we find the prices of fourteen principal articles of trade have been as follows:—

		1782-1800.	1801-20.	1821-50.	1851-70.	1871-80.	1881-84.
Beef, cwt.	s.	31	51	42	48	60	70
Butter, cwt.	s.	61	94	79	93	110	102
Coal, ton	s.	15	13	10	9	12	9
Coffee, cwt.	s.	99	110	66	57	88	72
Copper, cwt.	s.	96	143	94	93	76	67
Cotton, cwt.	s.	177	130	64	104	66	58
Flax, cwt.	s.	43	70	41	50	49	40
Iron, ton	s.	92	138	97	63	74	52
Lead, cwt.	s.	20	30	19	22	21	13
Sugar, cwt.	s.	41	45	33	32	26	19
Tallow, cwt.	s.	47	68	41	47	40	39
Timber, load	s.	52	110	62	63	56	51
Wheat, bushel	d.	89	130	85	80	71	58
Wool, lb.	d.	44	91	29	20	14	12

There was a remarkable rise of prices during the epoch of the Buonaparte wars, nearly 40 per cent. over the previous twenty years, that is, after allowing for the difference between gold and currency, the above prices being in gold. After Waterloo there was a steady decline until 1850, when prices again rose until 1864, as already stated (page 2), and in the last twenty years the downward tendency has only been checked at brief intervals.

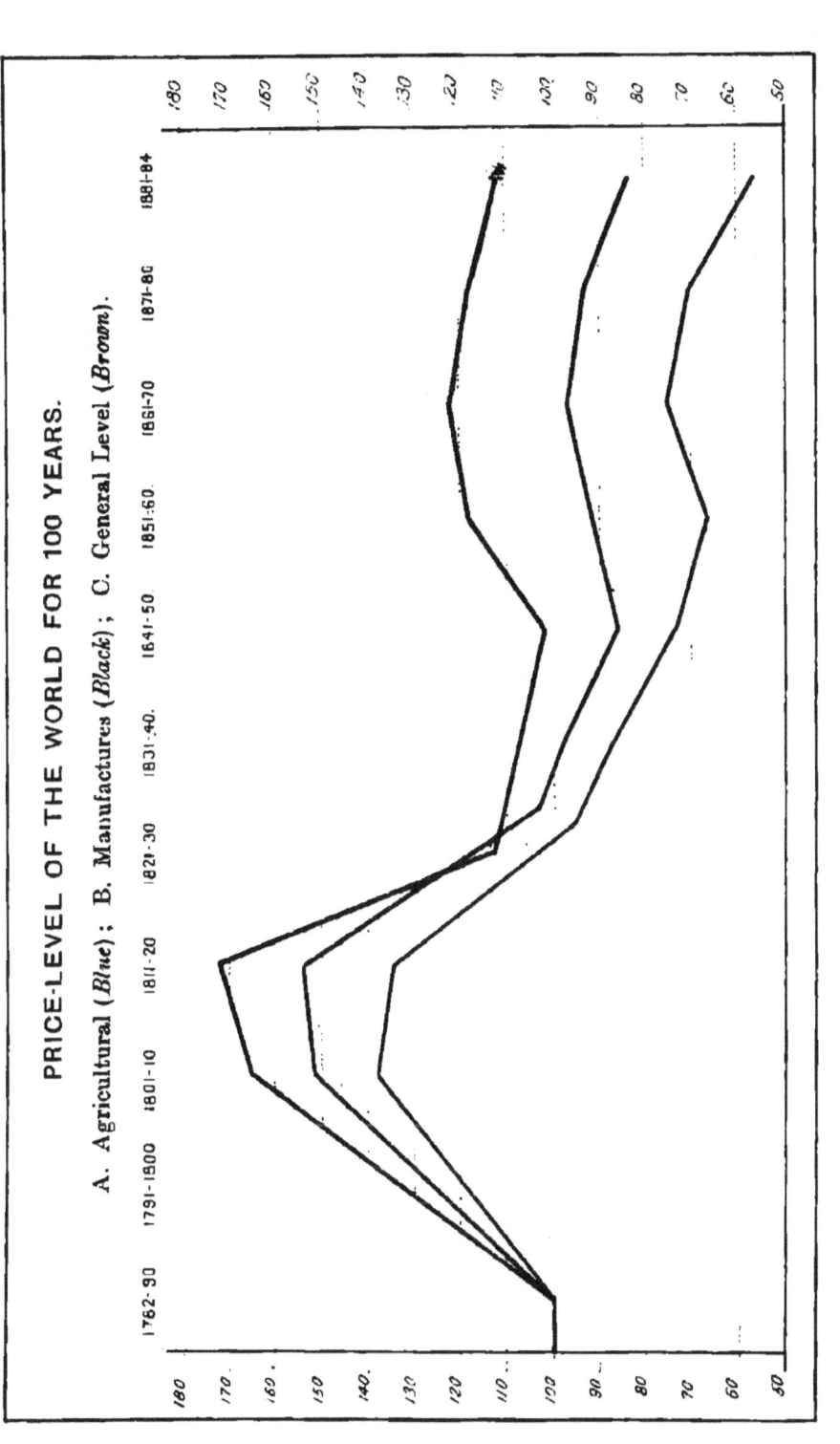

The rise in agricultural products in the years 1800-20 was almost twice as great as in manufactures, the former attaining their maximum in the Waterloo decade, whereas the latter were highest in the preceding one, as appears from the following statement :—

Volume of World's Merchandise for 1881-84 at Previous Prices.

	Millions £ Sterling.			Price-Level.		
Years.	Agri-cultural.	Indus-trial.	Total.	Agri-cultural.	Indus-trial.	Gene-ral.
1782–1790	2,773	3,142	5,915	100·0	100·0	100·0
1791–1800	3,653	3,637	7,290	131·8	115·8	123·3
1801–1810	4,607	4,344	8,951	166·1	138·2	151·7
1811–1820	4,754	4,282	9,036	171·5	136·3	152·7
1821–1830	3,139	2,974	6,113	113·2	94·6	103·4
1831–1840	3,012	2,744	5,756	108·6	87·3	97·4
1841–1850	2,826	2,360	5,186	102·0	75·1	87·7
1851–1860	3,272	2,157	5,429	118·0	68·6	91·8
1861–1870	3,416	2,346	5,762	123·2	74·6	97·4
1871–1880	3,293	2,186	5,479	118·8	69·6	92·7
1881–1884	3,133	1,777	4,910	113·0	56·6	83·0

The various items, agricultural and industrial, that make up the above table will be found *in extenso* in Appendix. The result may be summed up in these words :—With 11 shillings of present money we can buy as much manufactured goods as with 20 shillings a hundred years ago ; but as regards agricultural products, the £ sterling of to-day goes no further than 17½ shillings of that epoch. On the whole, 20 shillings in 1884 go as far as 24 shillings a century ago.

As regards wages, we find the averages in England have been :—

	Shillings per Week.				Ratio.		
	1780.	1820.	1840.	1880.	1780.	1840.	1880.
Blacksmith	17	24	21	32	100	124	190
Mason	17	25	23	35	100	136	206
Carpenter	15	20	20	30	100	133	200
Plumber	18	25	22	35	100	122	195
Spinner	12	16	18	24	100	150	200
Bailiff	8	12	15	20	100	188	250
Shepherd	6	8	10	15	100	167	250

If we compare the above wages with what they would buy, we find that the earnings of a carpenter, for example, would buy as follows:—

	Per Week.				Cost, Pence.			
	1780.	1820.	1840.	1880.	1780.	1820.	1840.	1880.
Beef, lbs..	10	10	12	16	30	50	50	130
Butter, ,, .	5	5	6	8	30	50	50	96
Sugar, ,, .	5	5	7	8	22	24	28	22
Wheat, ,,	70	70	80	100	80	100	100	100
Coal, cwt. .	2	2	2	2	18	16	12	12
					180	240	240	360

The English working man is therefore able to buy 44 per cent. more of the necessaries of life for his week's wages than he could a hundred years ago, and 21 per cent. more than in 1840. On the other hand, house-rent has trebled, for we find that the average for Great Britain in 1800 was barely £8 per house, and in 1881 it had risen to £21. After allowing for rent, it would still seem that the workman can buy 20 per cent. more than in 1780, and 10 per cent. more than in 1840.

Agricultural labourers in the eighteenth century received in England wages equivalent to a peck of wheat, that is, 14 lbs., and in France 12 lbs. ($\frac{1}{20}$th of a septier) daily. If we measure the earnings of farm labourers in 1880-82 in wheat we find as follows:—

Lbs. Wheat Daily.

Great Britain	25	Russia	. 11	Belgium	. 18
France	. 22	Austria	. 18	Scandinavia.	13
Germany	. 16	Italy .	. 11	Europe	. 17

It appears, therefore, that, measured by this standard, the rural peasantry earn 80 per cent. more than in the last century.

Some of the peasantry of Continental countries seem still poorly paid, but, compared with the product of their industry, their labour is much dearer than in England. Taking the working year at 300 days, and computing the wages of the farm labourer in each country, as well as the number of bushels of wheat he produces, we find the year's pay compares to product as follows :—

	Per Cent.		Per Cent.		Per Cent.
Great Britain	25	Russia	. 38	United States	18
France	. 53	Austria	. 55	Canada	. 30
Germany	. 36	Italy .	. 40	Europe	. 40

We see here that the production of grain in United States costs less than half what it costs in Europe as regards wages.

The principal points of this chapter are as follows :—

First. That £3 now will buy as much in England as £4 would a hundred years ago.

Secondly. That wages in England have doubled since 1780, and that working-men can buy 44 per cent. more of food than they could then, notwithstanding the enormous rise in beef and butter.

Thirdly. That house-rent having trebled in the same interval, the advantages to workmen in cities are sensibly reduced.

Fourthly. That the peasant's earnings, measured in grain, are 80 per cent. higher than in the eighteenth century.

Fifthly. That farm wages, compared with grain product, are 18 per cent. in United States, 25 per cent. in Great Britain, and 44 per cent. on the Continent.

XXII.

CAUSES THAT AFFECT PRICES.

The wars of Buonaparte drove up prices of agricultural products 72 per cent., and those of manufactured goods 38 per cent., as seen in the preceding chapter. Again, there was a rise consequent on the wars of 1851–60 (namely, the Crimean and Solferino campaigns and the Indian Mutiny), when agricultural prices rose 16 per cent., and the general price-level of the world showed an advance of 5 per cent. In the third place, the American War of 1861–64 had such effect that prices rose 78 per cent. in the United States and 52 per cent. in Great Britain over the level of 1841–50; and taking the whole decade of 1861–70, we find that its level was for the whole world 21 per cent. higher in agricultural products, and 11 per cent. higher for the general level of all merchandise, than the decade ending 1850. It is impossible, therefore, to doubt Tooke's theory that "war has a tendency to raise prices, by obstructing or diminishing the supply of commodities."

The peace that succeeded Waterloo saw prices fall nearly 50 per cent., the world's level for the decade ending 1830 being 33 per cent. less than the average of 1811–20. In like manner there was a steady decline after the war in the United States, the decade of 1871–80 for the world being 5 per cent. under the preceding, and we have had a continuous fall of prices since the Franco-German War. In a word, peace restores the level or the natural tendency of prices that was disturbed by war. But it does something more, by furthering arts and sciences, which tend to a lower level, for, as Newmarch says, " the tendency of all scientific discoveries and improvements is to cheapness."

Commerce directly leads to a lower level, although it gives enhanced value in particular countries which formerly had no market; thus, for example, fruit in Italy is worth four times what it was in the decade ending 1860, but the price of oranges in Europe has fallen from 11 to 7 shillings per bushel—a decline of 36 per cent.—and the customs-value of all imported fruit in Great Britain from £20 to £14 per ton in the same interval—a depression of 30 per cent. The trade-currents, which level barriers between nations, have precisely the opposite effects of war, and promote a lower level, to the general advantage of both producers and consumers.

Steam-power, as we have seen, exercises a prodigious influence in the same direction; for, as five men now perform as much work (p. 57) as eight could do in 1850, there is a saving of 40 per cent. of labour, and as labour constitutes one-third of the value of an article, we have herein a saving of 13 per cent. in the market price.

Improved facilities for transport also effect a great saving. We have seen (p. 48) that in 1850 the land-carriage of merchandise in Europe was six times what it is at present; in fact, the carriage of goods for 100 miles added 21 per cent. to their value, whereas transport by railway now adds only 5 per cent. for the same distance. At the same time freights by sea have fallen one-half, so that we have a saving of 5 to 10 per cent. in the value of merchandise before it reaches the consumer.

Another remarkable saving is in the cost of production of raw material, for we find that since 1870 wool has fallen 20, raw cotton 42, per cent.; and if we consider raw material as one-third of the value of any commodity, we have here sufficient reason for a decline of 7 per cent. in the price of woollens and 14 per cent. in cotton goods.

Scientific inventions, immediately bearing on particular branches of industry, have no less striking influence. We can now produce 3 tons of pig-iron at the same expenditure of coal that 2 tons took thirty years ago, and we can sell 3 tons of steel for less than 1 would have cost at that time. An economy of 33 per cent. in the whole range of hardware merchandise has powerfully contributed to the present lower price-level among nations, which is erroneously called trade depression.

Emigration has helped still further to cheapen the products of human industry by turning to immense advantage in newer parts of the world those energies and powers that could not find adequate field for exertion in Europe. If so monstrous a thing could be supposed as that the 15 million emigrants (1851–84) were now soldiers in European armies, instead of thriving settlers in America and Australia, the prices of wool and wheat would be 10 or 20 per cent. higher than they are.

There are numerous minor causes, such as electric telegraphs, reduced rates of discount, increasing competition among nations, improved methods of banking, more general use of cheques, and, in one word, a saving of time and expense between the producer and consumer of any commodity, all which point in the same direction.

The wonder is, not that the world's price-level for 1881–84 is 15 per cent. lower than that of 1861–70, but that it has not declined much more. We have, however, good reason to expect a slow, steady, and continuous fall of prices during the remainder of the nineteenth century if the peace of Europe be not seriously disturbed.

Popular delusions regarding prices are deep-rooted in the

CAUSES THAT AFFECT PRICES. 137

bulk of mankind, and we cannot be surprised that they prevail even in England to such a degree that nine Englishmen of every ten regard low prices as a calamity, and would apparently welcome a rise in the markets, procceding from no matter what circumstances. They do not see that high prices are a fool's paradise, where everybody seems to earn more, but is really no better off. Could we go back to the times when calico was worth 26 pence a yard, steel pens a shilling a piece, and wool 4 shillings per lb., when the quartern loaf cost 10 pence, should we find ourselves better or worse off? The farmer has no right to expect 100 shillings per quarter for wheat unless he be prepared to pay double his actual rent for the land and forego every advantage that the general fall of prices has conferred on society. No more penny newspapers, no more sixpenny telegrams, no more cheap hardware, implements, or machinery; everybody would require more income to keep pace with the rise of prices, and nobody would be any richer.

In the United States there is a much higher price-level than in Great Britain; a cab-driver charges 8 shillings for the shortest distance in New York City, or eight times the European average. Yet the result is the same in the end, and the cost of living is so high that even the street scavenger who earns a dollar a day is no better off than if his wages were two shillings under a European price-level. A Boston merchant recently stated to a group of passengers on a Cunard steamer that it paid him to come over to London to buy his clothes in England. An official at Washington has declared that he would rather have a salary of 2000 dollars a year in England than 4000 in the United States. Perhaps there can be no more evident example of the ineffectual nature of high price-levels than the island of Santo Domingo; the ordinary charges are in dollars, but happily of so depreciated a currency that it takes 600 of them to make 4 shillings; and although you pay a boatman or street-porter 50 dollars for any trifling service, he is no richer than if his pay were sixpence. The case would be no different if everybody were paid in gold, with an artificial price-level, as when the gold-diggers in California were paid £1 of English money daily, and eggs were worth 6 shillings dozen.

Another delusion, which has supporters among the most distinguished men in Great Britain, is that prices depend more or less on the stock of gold in the world, or on the question of bi-metallism. Two arguments ought to suffice to show the absurdity of such a theory. In the first place, only 48 per cent. of the actual stock of gold is used for money, the uncoined reserve being 768 millions sterling, against 425 millions in 1850, and hence the fall in prices cannot arise from any scarcity of that metal. In the second place, while the productive power (page 56) and volume of the world's products have risen 104 per cent. since 1850, the stock of gold has increased 140 per cent. (page 12); apart from the consideration that the use of cheques and bills of exchange has in a manner doubled the stock of gold, for we have already seen (page 14) that international commerce makes £5 go as far now as £12 of the precious metals in 1861-65. If the superabundant increase of both gold and silver found us at present with a higher level of prices than in 1850, there might be some excuse for the delusion, but the reverse is the case.

XXIII.

REVIEW OF BRITISH TRADE.

THE Appendix contains a complete price-list of one hundred articles of British imports and exports for the last thirty-one years, showing, moreover, the years of highest and lowest price for each distinct article, as well as one hundred index numbers, by which the relative rise or fall of the various commodities is indicated. On the following page is a synopsis of the said list, which places in a glance before the reader the whole current of trade since 1854, some points of which call for remark.

In the years 1854-57 there were thirty-four articles attained prices which have never since been reached, that is to say, one-third of the items of trade have steadily declined since 1857, and of these items twenty-one are imports and thirteen exports.

In the interval from 1857 to 1864 there was such an even flow of commerce that prices remained almost uniform, but in the latter year another rise occurred, by which twenty-eight articles (in the years 1864-68) reached unprecedented figures, from which they have since fallen back, never again reaching the level of those years; eleven were imports and seventeen exports. In a word, 67 per cent. of the articles forming British trade ranged at higher prices before 1868 than since.

A third rise occurred in 1873-74, by which fourteen articles attained prices not equalled before nor since, ten being exports and only four imports. If we sum up the result since 1854 we shall find that the greatest rise in imports was during and immediately following the Crimean War, and in exports about the close of the American and the

Franco-German Wars. The year in which the greatest number of articles of trade reached a maximum price was 1857.

On the other hand, we find that in 1884 there were thirty-five articles at prices so low that they were unprecedented. This depression of value may be said to have commenced in 1879, when eleven articles touched bathos. In fact, 61 per cent. of the items that constitute British trade have been since 1879 at lower prices than before recorded. The following table shows the number of articles in each year that touched highest or lowest prices between 1854 and 1884:—

	Highest.			Lowest.		
	Imports.	Exports.	Total.	Imports.	Exports.	Total.
1854	5	4	9	6	6	12
1855	4	2	6	1	2	3
1856	4	2	6	0	0	0
1857	8	5	13	1	0	1
1858	0	0	0	1	0	1
1859	0	1	1	1	0	1
1860	1	0	1	0	0	0
1861	0	0	0	0	0	0
1862	1	0	1	2	1	3
1863	2	0	2	1	1	2
1864	1	8	9	3	0	3
1865	1	2	3	2	1	3
1866	3	4	7	1	0	1
1867	1	3	4	1	0	1
1868	5	0	5	1	1	2
1869	2	1	3	1	0	1
1870	1	1	2	1	1	2
1871	0	0	0	0	0	0
1872	0	1	1	0	0	0
1873	1	7	8	0	0	0
1874	3	3	6	0	0	0
1875	0	1	1	0	1	1
1876	1	1	2	0	0	0
1877	0	0	0	0	0	0
1878	2	0	2	1	1	2
1879	1	0	1	7	4	11
1880	0	0	0	1	0	1
1881	0	1	1	1	3	4
1882	1	0	1	3	2	5
1883	1	0	1	2	3	5
1884	1	3	4	12	23	35
Total	50	50	100	50	50	100

REVIEW OF BRITISH TRADE.

Any deductions drawn from the above table with the view of showing that British trade has been in a ruinous condition since 1879 would be puerile absurdities. Some people may suffer by the change of price-level, but the community has grown in wealth, and commerce continues to increase not only in volume but in nominal amount of value. Dividing the whole period since 1855 into periods of three years, we find the following annual averages according to Board of Trade returns, and also the value according to price-level of 1841-50 :—

Millions Sterling per Annum.

Years.	Board of Trade.	Scale of 1841-50.	Years.	Board of Trade.	Scale of 1841-50.
1855-57	280	261	1870-72	556	497
1858-60	313	298	1873-75	611	531
1861-63	363	308	1876-78	577	576
1864-66	452	318	1879-81	607	645
1867-69	472	386	1882-84	648	715

There has been a steady uninterrupted increase of trade since 1854; for although the high level of prices in 1873-75 in a manner disturbed the stream of British commerce, and caused the years next succeeding to appear as if there was a decline, the scale of 1841-50 shows that at no period has there been any check or diminution. One particular year may be less than its predecessor, but it is safer to measure the growth in periods of three years, as in the above table.

The trade of the United Kingdom has risen 140 millions sterling since 1870, an increase unequalled in any other country of the world.

In order the better to understand the currents of trade, we may sum up the dealings of the United Kingdom with all foreign nations and our Colonies for twenty-four years as follows :—

142 HISTORY OF PRICES.

	Imports from, Millions £.				Exports to, Millions £.			
	1861–70.	1871–80.	1881–84.	Total.	1861–70.	1871–80.	1881–84.	Total.
France	298	421	155	874	230	283	115	628
Germany	162	217	100	479	261	334	122	717
Russia	169	200	72	441	69	101	34	204
Holland	110	175	99	384	145	193	65	403
Belgium	71	131	57	259	68	128	58	254
Scandinavia	76	137	65	278	36	76	31	143
Spain & Portugal	77	131	58	266	55	65	30	150
Other countries	116	135	64	315	133	183	75	391
Europe	1,079	1,547	670	3,296	997	1,363	530	2,890
United States	360	773	378	1,511	233	299	145	677
S. America	180	202	66	448	153	185	88	426
China & Japan	113	132	45	290	54	78	31	163
Egypt	158	114	37	309	60	40	13	113
India	345	299	144	788	197	241	127	565
Australia	103	201	106	410	128	188	106	422
Canada	75	108	45	228	60	87	40	187
Other countries	288	338	136	762	247	298	125	670
Total	2,701	3,714	1,627	8,042	2,129	2,779	1,205	6,113

In the whole period of twenty-four years the excess of imports averaged 80 millions sterling per annum, or 32 per cent. over and above the value of exports.

Looking back during the last thirty-five years to see how the commerce and industry of Great Britain have affected the well-being of the community, we find as follows:—

Year.	Millions.			Per Inhabitant, £.		
	Income-Tax Assessments.	Legacy Returns.	House Rental.	Income-Tax Assessments.	Legacy Returns.	House Rental.
1850	274	55	44	10	2·0	1·6
1860	335	63	58	11	2·1	2·0
1870	445	88	75	14	2·8	2·5
1880	578	119	114	17	3·5	3·3
1883–4	612	—	122	17	—	3·4

Each inhabitant of the United Kingdom possesses 70 per cent. more income than in 1850, as appears from the assessments to income-tax, which are further confirmed by the legacy returns. The valuation of house rental is perhaps more conclusive than the other two, as the wealth of a people is directly in ratio with the character of their dwellings. Each inhabitant pays now more than double the house rent that he paid in 1850; and if we go back no further than

REVIEW OF BRITISH TRADE.

1870 there is an improvement of 36 per cent. in these fourteen years, not from any artificial rise in value, but from the large amount of capital that has gone into building since 1870.

There are two other tests, namely, the savings-banks and the consumption of food, as follows :—

Year.	Savings-Banks.		Consumption per Inhabitant.			
	Millions Sterling.	Shillings per Inhab.	Sugar, lbs.	Meat, lbs.	Wheat, lbs.	Tea, oz.
1850	30	21	25	76	290	29
1860	41	29	32	86	320	43
1870	53	34	49	94	330	61
1880	77	44	68	101	335	73
1884	90	50	72	105	340	78

The consumption of food is the best of all measures of a nation's prosperity, and in this respect each year sees an improvement in the United Kingdom. It is doubly significant to notice that the consumption of meat per head has risen 40 per cent. since 1850, notwithstanding the great advance in price.

From the foregoing facts we have undoubted proof that the commerce of the United Kingdom has been, and continues to be, prosperous ; that it is closely connected with the public fortune ; and that the condition of the masses is improving.

For the benefit of those persons who wish to have the result of index numbers, the following summary shows the totals of fifty British imports and fifty exports, according to the detailed tables in Appendix :—

	Imports.	Exports.	Totals.
1854–60	5,000	5,000	10,000
1861–70	5,024	5,077	10,101
1871–80	4,902	4,882	9,784
1881–84	4,627	4,252	8,879
1854	4,823	4,936	9,759
1884	4,447	4,153	8,600

If price-level were determined by index numbers we should find a decline of 14 per cent. from the level of 1854–60, that is, of 17 per cent. in exports and 11 per cent. in imports.

XXIV.

CHRONICLE OF EVENTS.

The following summary of events in the last thirty-five years which may have affected prices, and some of which did so in a signal manner, will be useful for reference :—

1850.

Failure of cotton crop in United States: prices rose 80 per cent.; wheat dearer than in England.

Thousands of emigrants flocking to the new gold-fields in California.

First steam-plough in England, on Lord Willoughby D'Eresby's estate in Lincolnshire.

Agricultural depression; petition to the House of Commons by distressed land-owners and farmers.

Improvement of trade and revenue in the United Kingdom.

Parliament abolishes brick-duty and reduces window-tax.

British Colonies receive constitutional government.

1851.

Disraeli's bill to tax foreign grain defeated by fourteen votes.

Great Exhibition in Hyde Park, $6\frac{1}{4}$ million visitors.

Gold discovered at Bathurst, New South Wales, May 20th.

Commission in Paris to report on depreciation of gold.

Fears that the Bank of England must fail if compelled to pay 77¾ shillings per ounce for gold.

First line of steamers to Australia.

Petition of Liverpool shipowners to restore the Navigation Laws.

American reaping-machine, by Hussey, cut fifteen acres of wheat in twelve hours near Gateshead, saving 5 shillings an acre.

Silver rose to 62 pence per ounce, or 3 per cent. premium.

1852.

Alarm of French invasion; navy and artillery increased.
Fisheries dispute with United States.
Disraeli's budget thrown out; triumph of Free Trade.
French 5 per cents converted into $4\frac{1}{2}$ stock.
Famine in parts of Germany.
Land rising in value in England.
French Empire re-established.

1853.

Gladstone's budget, extending income-tax to Ireland.

Steam-plough with 2 horses and 10 men does work of 120 men.

Michel Chevalier's alarm about depreciation of gold.
New York papers deny any visible depreciation.
Calcutta Exchange, silver rupee 25 pence.
Russia invades the Danubian Principalities.

1854.

Holland demonetizes gold (law soon after repealed).
War in the Crimea.
United States treaty of commerce with Japan.
Lord Elgin's treaty for free trade between United States and Canada.

K

Increase of income-tax.
French loan for war expenses.

1855.

British war loan for 16 millions sterling.
Capture of Sebastopol.
Turkish loan for 5 millions sterling.
Rise of trade and revenue in United States.
Limited Liability Act passed by Parliament.

1856.

Prosperous times in Great Britain.
End of Crimean War.
Lord Canning annexed Oude.
War with China.

1857.

Great mutiny in India.
Redemption of Sound dues.
Crisis in United States and Great Britain; suspension of Bank Act; rate of discount raised to 10 per cent.
Several banks in England stopped payment; bullion reserve in Bank of England fell to £6,484,000.

1858.

Great Britain assumed the government of India.
Depression after crisis of last year; capital abundant, prices low.
Machine-reaper costs 50 per cent. of hand-labour, or 5 shillings per acre; steam-plough 40 per cent. of horse-labour, or 8 shillings per acre.
Loan of 7 millions sterling for India.
Anti-slavery agitation in United States.

1859.

Another alarm of French invasion.
Income-tax raised to 13 pence per £.
French war loan of 20 millions sterling, covered five times.
Franco-Italian war against Austria.
France annexes Savoy and Nice.

1860.

Palmerston's fortifications, outlay of 11 millions sterling.
Cobden's treaty of commerce with France.
Brisk recovery of trade in England.
Paper-duties abolished by Parliament.
Pekin taken by Anglo-French forces.

1861.

War in United States on slavery question.
Emancipation of serfs in Russia.
Reformation of French finances by Fould.
Post-Office savings banks introduced in United Kingdom.

1862.

Cotton famine; distress in Lancashire.
Ironclads (Merrimac and Monitor) first used in United States.
Anglo-French expedition to Mexico.
President Lincoln calls out 600,000 men.

1863.

Prussia secedes from the German Diet at Frankfort.
Insurrection in Poland.
Ionian Islands ceded to Greece.
Maximilian proclaimed Emperor of Mexico.

1864.

Sleswig-Holstein annexed to Germany.
Abolition of Scheldt dues.
Florence made capital of Italy.
Enormous increase of trade in Great Britain.
War between Spain and Peru.

1865.

Inflation of trade continues; 300 new joint-stock companies.
Project to federalise Canada.
Assassination of President Lincoln.
United States debt amounts to 570 millions sterling.
Bessemer's steel saves Great Britain 6 millions sterling yearly.

1866.

Conclusion of American war; Alabama Claims.
Cattle-plague in England; 30,000 animals dying monthly.
Overend Gurney crisis; Bank Act suspended.
Bank rate at 10 per cent. from May until August.
Great rise in price of meat.
Austro-Prussian war, battle of Sadowa.
Italy suspends specie payments, emits paper money.

1867.

Deficient harvest; meat very dear.
Death of Emperor Maximilian.
Great Exhibition at Paris; 9 million visitors.
Dominion of Canada constituted.
Diamond-fields discovered in South Africa.

1868.

Great Britain still suffering from crisis of 1866.
Fenian alarm; special constables sworn in London.

CHRONICLE OF EVENTS. 149

War in Abyssinia, death of Theodorus.
Republic established in Spain.

1869.

British telegraph lines bought by Government.
Trade very dull; increase of pauperism.
Reaction against Free Trade by "Reciprocity" agitators.
Opening of Suez Canal, after thirteen years of labour.

1870.

First loan for New Zealand.
Strike of 10,000 workmen at Creuzot, France.
Franco-German war; fall of Napoleon III.
Victor Emmanuel seized Rome.
Prince Amadeo made King of Spain.

1871.

German army took Paris.
German Empire proclaimed at Versailles.
City of Chicago burnt down.
Opening of Mont Cenis tunnel.

1872.

Geneva award on Alabama Claims, £3,100,000.
New French loans for 240 millions sterling.
Thiers defeated on wool-duties.
Maximum yield of African diamond-fields; 4 millions sterling.
Trade of Great Britain prosperous.
Railways introduced into Japan.

1873.

Alarm about British coal-fields; coal rose 20 per cent.
Banking crisis at Berlin and Vienna.

New German gold coinage (1872–73); minted 51 millions sterling.
MacMahon succeeds Thiers as president.
Republic restored in Spain ; Amadeo expelled.
Great Exhibition at Vienna ; 7½ million visitors.

1874.

Strikes of iron and coal workers.
War in Ashantee.
Alfonso XII. proclaimed King of Spain.
Famine in Bengal.
Joseph Arch's agricultural strike.

1875.

Plimsoll Shipping Act passed.
Abolition of light-dues by Holland.
Report on Foreign Loan frauds.
British Government bought Suez Canal shares.

1876.

Bismarck sold 3000 tons old silver coin for 28 millions sterling.
Silver fell to 46 pence per ounce.
Goschen's mission for Egyptian bondholders.
End of the Carlist War.
Murder of the Sultan. Bulgarian atrocities.
Philadelphia Exhibition, 10½ million visitors.

1877.

Siege and capture of Plevna.
Gordon suppresses the Soudan slave-trade.
Jablochkoff's electric light used at Lyons.
Invention of the telephone.
Ravages by the Colorado beetle, United States.

1878.

Berlin Conference. Great Britain annexes Cyprus.
City of Glasgow Bank failed.
Paris Exhibition, 16 million visitors.
Bland Act passed for coining 24 million silver dollars yearly.

1879.

United States resume specie payments; revival of trade.
Distress in Great Britain, increase of pauperism.
Ismail Pasha removed from Egypt.
Revival of iron trade in England.
United States debts converted into 4 per cents.
Baron Lesseps undertakes the Panama Canal.

1880.

Deficit in Indian budget.
Overthrow of Conservatives, Gladstone premier.
Relief of Candahar by General Roberts.
Australia sends wheat and frozen meat to England.
Persecution of Jews in Germany.

1881.

Rumours of impending gold famine.
Agricultural depression in England.
Annexation of Tunis by the French.
Australian 6 per cents converted into 4 per cents.
Assassination of the Czar Alexander.

1882.

Financial difficulties in France.
Bombardment of Alexandria.
Irish Land Act passed by Parliament.
Enormous food-exports from United States.

1883.

French annexations in Madagascar and Tonquin.
General Hicks's army destroyed by the Mahdi.
Arabi Pasha banished to Ceylon.
Persecution of Jews in Russia.
Parliament prohibits the proposed Channel Tunnel.
King Alphonso mobbed in Paris.

1884.

Cholera at Toulon and Naples.
General Gordon holds Khartoum.
Annexation of Merv by Russia.
War between France and China.

1885.

Death of General Gordon; fall of Khartoum.
New Guinea annexed by Germany.
Democrat Cleveland elected President of the United States.
Advance of Russia towards Herat.
Fall of Gladstone Cabinet.
Cholera in Spain.
Carolinas question between Spain and Germany.

APPENDIX.

A.

Price-Levels of British Trade.

THE following table* shows the actual Board of Trade returns and the amounts that would have resulted for imports and exports if prices of 1841–50 had remained unchanged, in *millions sterling*.

Year.	Board of Trade.			Prices of 1841–50.		
	Imports.	Exports.	Total.	Imports.	Exports.	Total.
1854	152	97	249	140	102	242
1855	144	96	240	126	105	231
1856	173	116	289	149	125	274
1857	188	122	310	152	127	279
1858	165	117	282	150	125	275
1859	179	130	309	160	136	296
1860	211	136	347	180	143	323
1861	217	125	342	189	130	319
1862	226	124	350	193	114	307
1863	249	147	396	182	116	298
1864	275	160	435	173	114	287
1865	271	166	437	191	127	318
1866	295	189	484	208	140	348
1867	275	181	456	215	148	363
1868	295	180	475	235	157	392
1869	295	190	485	238	165	403
1870	303	200	503	280	179	459
1871	331	223	554	302	203	505
1872	355	256	611	323	205	528
1873	371	255	626	317	199	516
1874	370	240	610	328	201	529
1875	374	224	598	349	199	548
1876	375	201	576	371	196	567
1877	394	199	593	375	203	578
1878	369	193	562	380	202	582
1879	363	192	555	390	212	602
1880	411	223	634	423	239	662
1881	397	234	631	410	260	670
1882	413	242	655	435	260	695
1883	427	240	667	465	266	731
1884	390	233	623	459	259	718

* This table does not contain foreign and colonial merchandise exported from United Kingdom.

APPENDIX.

The ratio of values for the thirty-one years are summed up as follows, in comparison with the price-level of 1841–50, which is taken as 100.

Year.	Board of Trade.			Year.	Board of Trade.		
	Imports.	Exports.	Total.		Imports.	Exports.	Total.
1854 .	109	95	103	1871 .	110	110	110
1855 .	115	91	104	1872 .	110	125	116
1856 .	116	93	105	1873 .	117	128	121
1857 .	124	96	111	1874 .	113	120	115
1858 .	110	94	103	1875 .	107	112	109
1859 .	112	95	104	Average .	111	119	114
1860 .	117	95	107	1876 .	101	103	102
Average .	115	94	105	1877 .	105	98	103
1861 .	115	96	107	1878 .	97	95	96
1862 .	117	109	114	1879 .	93	91	92
1863 .	136	126	133	1880 .	97	93	96
1864 .	160	141	152	Average .	98	96	97
1865 .	142	131	138	1881 .	97	90	94
Average .	134	121	129	1882 .	95	93	94
1866 .	142	135	139	1883 .	92	90	91
1867 .	128	122	126	1884 .	85	90	87
1868 .	126	115	121	Average .	92	91	91½
1869 .	124	115	121	1861–70	130	121	126
1870 .	108	111	110	1871–80	105	108	106
Average .	126	120	123	1854–84 .	113½	107	110

Summary.

Imports of 1881–84 show a price-level 8 per cent. below that of 1841–50, exports 9 per cent.

The same imports are 20 per cent. below the level of 1854–60, and the exports only 3 per cent. less.

The same imports have fallen 30 per cent. from the price-level of 1861–70, the exports 25 per cent.

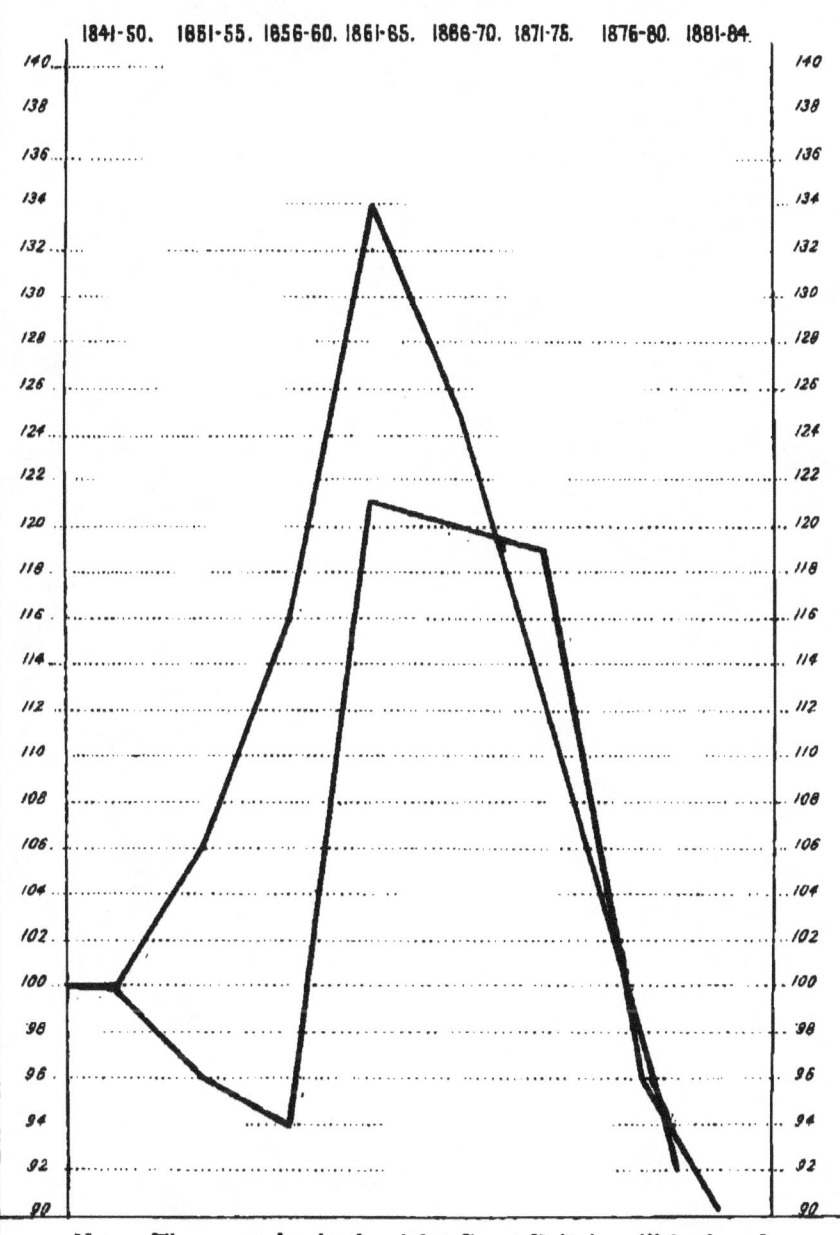

B.

PRICE-LEVELS FROM 1860–1883.

The following table shows the actual trade of the principal countries, in comparison with what the amounts would have been at the average of prices in 1860-62.

Trade Returns, Millions Sterling.

Year.	United Kingdom.*	France.	Italy.	Belgium.	United States.	Aggregate.
1860-62	346	180	54	41	101	722
1863	396	203	61	46	59	765
1864	435	218	62	51	46	812
1865	437	229	61	54	47	828
1866	484	239	59	56	82	920
1867	456	234	65	55	99	909
1868	475	244	67	61	92	939
1869	485	249	69	64	106	973
1870	503	227	66	64	144	1,004
Average	428	216	61	52	89	847
1871	554	258	81	87	175	1,155
1872	611	293	94	93	193	1,284
1873	626	294	96	103	207	1,326
1874	610	288	91	96	210	1,295
1875	598	296	89	96	184	1,263
1876	576	303	101	101	182	1,263
1877	593	284	83	100	206	1,266
1878	562	294	82	103	225	1,266
1879	555	313	93	109	236	1,306
1880	634	340	91	116	308	1,489
Average	592	296	90	100	213	1,291
1881	631	337	96	117	314	1,495
1882	655	336	95	117	300	1,503
1883	667	330	99	116	312	1,524

* See note on p. 153.

APPENDIX.

At Prices of 1860–62, Millions Sterling.

Year.	U.K.	France.	Italy.	Belgium.	U.S.	Aggregate.
1863	328	197	60	49	65	699
1864	315	204	62	53	43	677
1865	347	225	57	58	45	732
1866	381	244	60	58	48	791
1867	396	273	61	61	100	891
1868	432	280	64	70	86	932
1869	445	286	65	79	85	960
1870	503	283	63	75	133	1,057
Average	393	249	61	63	76	842
1871	554	310	77	90	156	1,187
1872	599	338	80	88	154	1,259
1873	570	330	78	100	207	1,285
1874	586	348	85	97	206	1,322
1875	604	380	93	99	192	1,368
1876	618	379	93	109	214	1,413
1877	631	368	83	103	204	1,389
1878	648	387	89	112	271	1,507
1879	657	391	96	122	262	1,528
1880	737	420	101	121	321	1,700
Average	620	366	87	104	219	1,396
1881	742	431	110	123	334	1,740
1882	770	442	116	141	306	1,775
1883	794	463	129	149	343	1,883
Average	769	445	118	138	328	1,798

Ratio of Values.

Year.	U.K.	France.	Italy.	Belgium.	U.S.	General.
1860–62	100	100	100	100	100	100
1863	121	103	101	94	90	109
1864	138	107	100	96	106	120
1865	126	102	107	92	104	113
1866	127	98	98	97	170	116
1867	115	86	107	90	99	102
1868	110	87	105	87	107	101
1869	109	87	106	81	125	101
1870	100	80	105	85	108	95
Average	118	94	104	90	114	107
1871	100	83	106	97	112	97
1872	106	87	118	105	125	102
1873	110	89	122	103	100	103
1874	104	83	107	99	102	97
1875	99	78	96	97	96	92
1876	93	80	109	93	85	89
1877	94	77	100	97	101	91
1878	87	76	92	92	83	84
1879	84	80	97	89	90	85
1880	86	81	90	96	96	88
Average	96	81	104	97	99	92
1881	85	78	87	95	94	86
1882	85	76	82	83	98	85
1883	84	71	77	78	91	81
Average	85	75	82	85	94	84

C.

PRECIOUS METALS.

Gold Coinage of all Nations (in Millions Sterling) from 1850 to 1883 inclusive.

	Total Coined.	Re-minted.	Net Increase.	Existing Coin in 1884–85.	Amount in 1850.
Great Britain	155 } 138		82	147	65
British Colonies	65 }				
France	299	117	182	198	16
Germany	91	26	65	75	10
Russia	110	86	24	30	6
Austria	14	7	7	10	3
Italy	17	4	13	30	17
Spain and Portugal	31	8	23	38	15
Belgium and Holland	29	9	20	26	6
Scandinavia	5	2	3	5	2
United States	254	158	96	130	34
Total	1,070	555	515	689	174

Other nations, including Switzerland, Greece, Servia, Roumania, Turkey, Egypt, Persia, Japan, Spanish America, &c., have 47 millions, bringing up the grand total of existing gold coin to 736 millions sterling.

Current of Gold (in Millions Sterling.)

	Imported.			Exported.		
By	1861–70.	1871–83.	23 Years.	1861–70.	1871–83.	23 Years.
Great Britain	171	212	383	112	206	318
France	189	176	365	119	114	233
United States	31	73	104	113	83	196
Australia	9	12	21	108	95	203
Other countries	112	164	276	60	139	199
Total	512	637	1,149	512	637	1,149

APPENDIX.

Quantity of Silver Plate Stamped in Great Britain, Annual Average.

Years.	Oz., 000's omitted.	Years.	Oz., 000's omitted.
1801–10	1,087	1841–50	1,007
1811–20	1,058	1851–60	930
1821–30	1,157	1861–70	875
1831–40	1,104	1871–80	790

The consumption of silver plate in France has risen slightly; it averaged 2,100,000 oz. in 1851–60, and 2,300,000 in 1861–70, the decade ending 1880 showing 2,400,000 ounces per annum.

Wear and Tear of Metals.

The loss in weight of gold coin being 2 per cent. in a hundred years (Jevons), and the actual stock 736 millions sterling, the annual wear and tear is just 1 ton, or £147,000 sterling. Add £101,000 for loss by shipwreck, £32,000 for fires, and the total annual loss comes to 2 tons, the actual stock of gold coined and uncoined being 11,000 tons.

The loss of silver is 200 tons yearly, or 1 per 1000, that is, five times greater than that of gold.

Stocks of Gold and Silver.

A.D.	Tons.		Silver to Gold.
	Gold.	Silver.	
1600	750	22,800	30 to 1
1700	1,660	60,000	36 ,, 1
1800	3,570	117,000	33 ,, 1
1850	4,750	148,000	32 ,, 1
1885	10,760	201,000	19 ,, 1

The above comprises all the precious metals existing in the world, coined or uncoined.

APPENDIX.

Production of Gold.

Millions Sterling.

Year.	U. States.	Australia.	Russia.	Various.	Total.
1849	1·8	...	3·6	4·0	9·4
1850	5·5	...	3·4	4·1	13·0
1851	8·8	1·0	4·0	3·8	17·6
1852	10·2	10·2	4·0	3·5	27·9
1853	11·0	11·2	3·4	3·6	29·2
1854	12·2	9·4	3·4	3·9	28·9
1855	11·0	12·0	3·5	4·1	30·6
1856	11·6	13·2	3·5	4·0	32·3
1857	10·4	11·6	4·2	3·8	30·0
1858	9·8	12·1	4·2	3·7	29·8
1859	9·2	12·2	4·0	3·8	29·2
1860	8·0	11·2	4·0	3·9	27·1
1861	10·7	9·6	4·0	4·0	28·3
1862	10·4	9·7	4·0	4·0	28·1
1863	11·4	9·0	3·8	4·2	28·4
1864	9·0	7·6	3·9	4·2	24·7
1865	9·4	7·4	3·9	4·4	25·1
1866	9·5	7·8	4·0	4·4	25·7
1867	8·8	7·6	4·0	4·6	25·0
1868	9·4	8·0	4·1	4·6	26·1
1869	10·2	8·0	4·2	4·8	27·2
1870	9·0	7·6	4·2	4·8	25·6
1871	8·0	8·0	4·2	4·8	25·0
1872	5·2	8·4	4·5	4·8	22·9
1873	6·8	10·0	4·6	5·0	26·4
1874	7·0	8·8	4·6	5·0	25·4
1875	7·4	7·6	4·7	5·2	24·9
1876	7·8	6·5	4·7	5·2	24·2
1877	8·0	8·3	5·0	5·0	26·3
1878	7·2	5·9	5·0	4·8	22·9
1879	6·1	4·0	5·2	4·6	19·9
1880	6·3	4·4	5·4	4·4	20·5
1881	6·9	4·3	5·6	3·0	19·8
1882	6·6	4·0	5·8	2·8	19·2
1883	6·1	4·4	6·0	2·7	19·2
1884	6·2	4·2	6·2	2·4	19·0
Total	302·9	275·2	156·8	149·9	884·8

D.

MONEY-MARKET.

Capital Employed in Banking.

	Millions Sterling.	Sum per Inhabitant, £ Sterling.	Amount in Savings Banks, Millions £.
United Kingdom	840	24	90
France	218	6	74
Germany	290	6	110
Russia	155	2	5
Austria	166	5	88
Italy	93	3	35
Switzerland	20	7	12
Spain and Portugal	22	1	3
Belgium and Holland	53	6	8
Scandinavia	35	4	27
Europe	1,892	6	452
United States	530	10	202
Australia	103	32	...
Canada	48	11	...
	2,573	7	654

Banking in United Kingdom (1882).

Banks.	Millions £.				
	Capital.	Issue.	Deposits.	Discounts.	Assets.
English	74	28	279	225	398
Scotch	15	6	79	62	105
Irish	10	7	23	20	20
Colonial	55	10	132	251	250
	154	51	513	558	785

APPENDIX.

Clearing-House Returns.

The daily average in millions sterling is as follows:—

| United States | 42 | London | 21 | Berlin | 3 |
| New York | 25 | Paris | 7 | Vienna | 2 |

Melbourne averages £500,000 and Manchester £400,000 daily.

The returns for London have been daily as follows:—

Year.	Millions Sterling.	Year.	Millions Sterling.
1839	3	1871-80	19
1867-70	11	1881-84	26

The use of cheques in ratio of payments is as follows:—

	Per Cent.		Per Cent.		Per Cent.
London	99	Provinces (Eng.)	68	Western States	82
England	97	New York	99	United States	92

The above returns are for the year 1881, the latest ascertained.

Number of Depositors in Savings Banks.

Year.	Great Britain.	Continent.	Europe.
1850	1,060,000	2,851,000	3,911,000
1860	1,580,000	5,115,000	6,695,000
1870	2,620,000	8,213,000	10,833,000
1881	3,715,000	15,360,000	19,075,000

E.

FINANCES.

The annual expenditure of nations in 1883–84 was as follows :—

Millions Sterling.

	Government.	Interest on Debt.	Military.	Total.
United Kingdom	30·4	29·7	28·9	89·0
France	58·5	51·1	32·0	141·6
Germany	65·4	11·0	27·0	103·4
Russia	38·1	24·4	29·5	92·0
Austria	34·6	23·7	12·6	70·9
Italy	25·1	24·5	12·4	62·0
Spain	17·2	11·0	6·8	35·0
Portugal	3·7	2·9	1·2	7·8
Belgium	6·7	4·1	2·0	12·8
Holland	5·1	2·3	2·6	10·0
Denmark	1·0	0·5	0·9	2·4
Sweden and Norway	4·3	1·0	1·8	7·1
Europe	290·1	186·2	157·7	634·0
United States	27·6	11·4	11·8	50·8
Canada	4·0	1·8	0·2	6·0
Australia	17·8	5·0	0·2	23·0
Brazil	4·7	3·7	3·0	11·4
Argentine Republic	2·4	3·2	2·2	7·8
Egypt	4·4	3·5	0·5	8·4
India	46·9	4·5	18·0	69·4
Japan	4·8	4·3	2·3	11·4
Total	402·7	223·6	195·9	822·2

APPENDIX.

Debts of Nations, in Millions Sterling.

	1718.	1763.	1793.	1816.	1848.	1870.	1884.
Great Britain	54	147	370	841	773	801	756
France	48	110	32	140	182	468	995
Germany	...	...	...	53	40	148	334
Russia	...	...	30	50	90	280	555
Austria	10	15	20	99	125	340	508
Italy	...	...	...	25	36	374	438
Spain	7	11	20	52	113	285	330
Portugal	...	...	1	8	17	59	107
Holland	...	...	70	110	114	76	84
Belgium	...	...	...	...	18	28	78
Denmark	...	...	...	4	12	13	12
Sweden and Norway	...	...	...	...	1	6	20
Greece	...	...	...	...	10	18	18
Turkey	...	...	...	...	...	92	148
Roumania	...	...	...	...	...	...	27
Servia	...	...	...	...	...	...	4
Europe	119	283	543	1,382	1,531	2,988	4,414
United States	...	...	17	26	48	496	305
Spanish America	...	...	...	...	17	135	195
Canada	...	...	...	...	...	17	38
Australia	...	...	...	...	...	37	116
India	...	...	9	29	51	108	160
Japan	...	...	...	...	2	10	67
Egypt	...	...	...	...	...	37	113
South Africa	...	...	...	...	...	2	23
The World	119	283	569	1,437	1,649	3,830	5,431

The reduction of French debt after 1763 was by its repudiation after the revolution of 1789.

F.

COMMERCE AND SHIPPING.

Amount of Imports to £100 of Exports.

	1861-70. £	1871-80. £		1861-70. £	1871-80. £
Great Britain	127	133	Europe	117	125
France	99	121	United States	136	88
Germany	140	137	Canada	123	129
Russia	96	102	Australia	151	118
Austria	86	113	India	56	62
Italy	138	107	China, &c.	104	107
Spain and Portugal	136	104	South America	104	90
Belgium	125	127	Egypt	40	39
Holland	123	146	Java	56	55
Scandinavia	113	133	The World	111	113

Comparative Table of British Trade and that of United States.

	British Trade. (Millions Sterling, Annual Average.)			American Trade.		
	Imports.	Exports.	Total.	Imports.	Exports.	Total.
1831-40	54	57	111	21	18	39
1841-50	83	75	158	22	22	44
1851-60	153	121	274	54	47	101
1861-70	270	213	483	47	36	83
1871-80	371	278	649	96	108	204
1881-84	407	302	709	134	157	291

	Customs Dues, Millions Sterling.		Percentage to Imports.		Trade per Inhabitant. £	
	British.	American.	British.	American.	G. Britain.	U. States.
1831-40	20	4	37	19	4·4	2·6
1841-50	23	5	27	23	5·8	2·2
1851-60	24	11	16	20	9·8	3·7
1861-70	22	17	8	36	16·1	2·4
1871-80	20	31	5¾	32	18·7	4·6
1881-84	19	41	4¾	31	20·2	5·6

APPENDIX.

In the above table British exports include Colonial goods in transit.

Internal Waters of United States.

Waters.	Number of Steamers.	Traffic, 000's omitted.	
		Passengers.	Goods, Tons.
Lakes	947	1,420	4,380
Mississippi	681	2,710	4,820
Ohio	473	4,030	2,410
Gulf	1,116	9,160	4,110
Coast	1,922	151,190	9,820
	5,139	168,510	25,540

The above returns are for the year 1880.

Suez Canal Traffic.

Year.	Vessels.	Tons.	Average Tonnage.
1870	486	436,000	900
1875	1,494	2,940,000	1,960
1882	3,198	7,122,000	2,225

Canal dues average 7 shillings per ton gross measurement.

British Shipping, Tons (000's omitted).

	Built.			Broken up or Lost.			Increased Tonnage.
	Steam.	Sailing.	Total.	Steam.	Sailing.	Total.	
1879	449	62	511	131	190	321	190
1880	486	60	546	118	220	338	208
1881	661	88	749	142	213	355	394
1882	790	138	928	163	210	373	555
1883	885	142	1,027	199	194	393	634
1884	568	161	729	192	174	366	363

Shipping Built by all Nations.

Years.	Tonnage (000's omitted) per Annum.			Percentage.	
	Steam.	Sailing.	Total.	Steam.	Sailing.
1851-60	63	635	698	9	91
1861-70	151	910	1,061	14	86
1871-83	637	735	1,372	46	54

Tonnage of Entries (1883).

Millions of Tons.

United Kingdom	32·1	Germany . .	7·1	Belgium . .	4·3
British Colonies	36·5	Italy . . .	5·7	Holland . .	4·0
United States	13·4	Austria . .	5·2	Portugal . .	3·1
France . .	13·7	Russia . .	4·7	China . . .	2·0
Spain . .	7·6	Sweden & Norway	6·6	S. America, &c. .	6·4

The above make up a total of 152 million tons.

Entries in United Kingdom.

	Millions of Tons.			
Year.	High-seas.	Coasting.	Total.	Tons. per inhab.
1840	4·7	12·6	17·3	0·7
1850	7·3	21·5	28·8	1·0
1860	12·3	24·4	36·7	1·2
1870	18·3	28·9	47·2	1·5
1880	29·1	36·1	65·2	1·9
1884	31·7	36·8	68·5	2·0

Entries in United States Ports.

	Millions of Tons.			
Year.	American.	British.	Other.	Total.
1860	3·3	1·3	0·4	5·0
1870	2·5	2·8	1·0	6·3
1884	2·8	8·5	3·4	14·7

G.

RAILWAYS.

Mileage Traffic, in Thousands
(17·9 = 17,900 Passengers).

	Passengers.			Goods, Tons.		
	1860.	1870.	1882.	1860.	1870.	1882.
Great Britain	17·9	22·4	41·1	7·9	10·8	14·2
France	9·3	10·2	10·6	3·7	4·8	5·5
Germany	7·0	11·4	9·9	3·5	8·3	7·1
Russia	4·7	2·1	2·6	2·8	1·2	2·4
Austria	4·0	3·6	3·7	2·4	4·2	4·8
Italy	5·8	6·2	6·1	0·9	1·5	1·9
Spain and Portugal	5·1	2·6	5·3	1·7	1·1	1·4
Belgium and Holland	14·9	18·0	17·9	6·6	11·2	10·2
Switzerland	8·8	16·4	13·8	1·5	4·4	3·9
Scandinavia	1·3	4·4	3·0	0·1	2·8	1·6
Europe	10·6	11·5	12·7	4·8	6·2	5·6
United States	...	2·1	2·9	...	2·9	3·9

Cost of Construction and Net Profit.

	Cost per Mile.	Profit on Capital.		Cost per Mile.	Profit on Capital.
England	49·2	4·2	Portugal	15·4	2·5
Scotland	33·3	3·7	Belgium	22·5	3·7
Ireland	14·2	3·6	Holland	18·6	3·5
United Kingdom	42·1	4·3	Denmark	10·3	2·1
France	27·4	4·1	Sweden & Norway	6·8	2·4
Germany	21·1	4·2	United States	11·1	4·4
Russia	20·5	2·2	Canada	9·6	1·8
Austria	20·7	3·8	Australia	10·4	3·6
Italy	19·4	2·5	India	14·6	4·6
Spain	16·4	3·8	General average	16·9	4·0

In 1882 the railways of the world carried 6 million passengers and 3 million tons merchandise daily, for which they received £1,200,000, no less than 2,400,000 persons being employed in their service.

H.

MANUFACTURES.

Cotton-Mills of all Nations.

	Spindles, Millions.	Operatives. Thousands.
Great Britain	40·2	482
United States	11·2	260
Germany	5·4	150
France	4·8	170
Russia	3·4	180
Austria	2·2	100
Spain	1·6	80
India	1·2	80
Belgium, &c.	4·3	141
Total	74·3	1,643

Silk Industry.

Year.	Consumption, Million lbs.	Manufactures, Millions Sterling.	Raw Silk, Shillings per lb.
1850	30	52	14
1860	33	60	21
1870	36	70	26
1880	38	73	17

	Annual Consumption, Million lbs. Raw Silk.		Value of Fabrics, Millions Sterling (1884).	
	1861–65.	1876–80.	Manufactures.	Consumption.
Great Britain	5·5	2·9	6·8	15·6
France	12·3	15·2	27·4	16·2
Germany	2·1	3·4	4·5	6·0
Russia	0·6	1·0	2·1	2·4
Austria	1·0	2·1	3·8	6·0
Italy	1·3	1·6	3·1	3·0
Spain, &c.	0·7	1·2	5·0	2·7
United States	0·5	1·8	5·5	12·1
China	9·0	9·0	15·0	11·2
	33·0	38·2	73·2	75·2

The production in 1880 was as follows:—

	Million lbs.
China	21·0
Japan	4·4
Italy	6·6
India, &c.	2·0
France, &c.	4·0
Total	38·0

Only one-tenth of the Italian crop is from native eggs, the rest being obtained from 70 tons of eggs yearly imported.

Linen Manufactures.

	Flax, Million lbs.	Spindles, 000's omitted.	Linen Fabrics, Millions Sterling.
United Kingdom	230	1,485	11·5
France	145	762	8·2
Germany	77	327	4·0
Russia	88	145	4·1
Austria	132	415	7·6
Belgium and Holland	66	296	3·8
Italy, &c.	22	64	1·2
United States	40	13	2·6
Total	800	3,507	43·0

Hemp.

	Production, Tons.
Austria	110,000
Italy	90,000
Russia	60,000
France	50,000
Holland, &c.	115,000
Total	425,000

Consumption in Great Britain.

Year.	Tons.	Value, £ per Ton.
1850	54,200	28
1860	35,200	30
1870	71,300	38
1880	73,400	28
1883	77,700	33

During the American War it went over £40 a ton, and afterwards fell steadily until 1880, since which year it has risen by degrees, apparently unaffected by the enormous increase of jute.

Woollen Manufactures (1880).

	Millions, lbs. Wool.	Manufactures, Millions Sterling.
United Kingdom	338	46·1
France	336	43·3
Germany	190	26·3
Russia	170	23·0
Austria	80	10·7
Belgium	93	7·8
Spain and Portugal	70	8·5
Italy, &c.	53	6·9
United States	320	43·0
Total	1,650	213·5

Co-operative Societies.

These societies have affected retail prices in the large towns, but cannot be said to have influenced wholesale prices. The first was established at Rochdale, Lancashire, in 1844 by twenty-eight workmen, with a capital of £28. Some of the London societies' shares are now worth a hundred times the original amount of subscription. There are in Great Britain 1,120 co-operative societies, with 1,100,000 members, whose joint-stock capital reaches seven millions sterling. The five principal London societies show sales amounting to £4,500,000 per annum; working expenses (including wages, rent, &c.), £250,000, equal to $5\frac{1}{2}$ per cent. on sales.

There are in Germany 3,120 co-operative societies, initiated by Mr. Schultz-Delitsch, counting 1,200,000 members, with an aggregate capital of 19 millions sterling; annual turnover, 140 millions sterling. These societies have grown so rapidly that in 1860 there were only 133, numbering 32,000 members.

I.

AGRICULTURE.

Acreage under Flax.

	1866-70.	1882-83.
United Kingdom	220,000	102,000
France	196,000	137,000
Austria	290,000	245,000
Russia	2,260,000	1,950,000
Germany	370,000	292,000
Belgium and Holland	210,000	126,000
Italy, &c.	260,000	244,000
United States	120,000	160,000
	3,926,000	3,256,000

Cultivation of Potatoes.

	000's omitted.		Cwts. per Acre.	Bushels per Inhabitant.
	Acres.	Crop, Tons.		
United Kingdom	1,379	4,840	70	5·3
France	3,200	9,500	59	9·2
Germany	8,800	23,300	52	19·1
Russia	3,100	9,200	60	4·0
Austria	3,500	8,100	46	9·1
Belgium, &c.	1,760	5,670	64	3·3
Europe	21,739	60,610	60	6·7
United States	1,900	3,500	37	2·5
Canada, &c.	1,100	3,300	60	...
Total	24,739	67,410	57	

Agriculture in the United States.

Year.	Farms, Millions of Acres.	Value, Millions Sterling.	Grain, Million Bushels.	Bushels per Inhabitant.
1850	293	683	868	37
1860	407	1,382	1,240	39
1870	410	1,923	1,388	36
1880	534	2,116	2,699	54

Agriculture in the United Kingdom.

Acres, 000's omitted.

	1868-69.			1884.			
	Great Britain.	Ireland.	United Kingdom.	England.	Scotland.	Ireland.	United Kingdom.
Wheat	3,690	283	3,973	2,608	69	69	2,746
Oats	2,750	1,720	4,470	1,870	1,046	1,347	4,263
Barley	2,203	170	2,373	1,938	231	167	2,336
Potatoes	528	1,037	1,565	401	164	799	1,364
Turnips	2,185	321	2,506	1,543	485	304	2,332
Sundries	1,794	2,017	3,811	1,562	56	135	1,753
Total	13,150	5,548	18,698	9,922	2,051	2,821	14,794

The area under crops has fallen 20 per cent., and the actual ratio of tillage is only 41 acres per 100 inhabitants, against 62 acres in 1868.

Vineyards and Wine Production in France.

Years.	Acres of Vines, 000's omitted.	Millions of Gallons Wine.	Gallons per Acre.	Export, Millions of Gallons.
1850-52	5,450	920	168	38
1860-62	5,510	703	126	48
1870-72	6,560	1,010	153	70
1880-82	5,150	720	140	55

Vineyards of all Nations.

	Acres, 000's omitted.	Millions of Gallons.	Gallons per Acre.	Pence per Gallon.
France	5,150	720	140	15
Italy	4,650	580	125	13
Spain	2,720	320	118	14
Portugal	420	80	190	30
Austria	1,580	310	196	12
Germany	305	70	230	14
Russia	110	19	170	24
Europe	14,935	2,099	133	14
United States	130	21	160	23
Algeria	51	9	176	20
Argentine Republic	60	6	105	28
South Africa	18	4	220	...
Australia	15	2	130	...
Chili	88	14	160	30
Other countries	100	15	150	...
Total	15,397	2,170	141	14

Hops.

	Acres.	Tons.	Value, £ Sterling.
England	67,100	26,200	3,120,000
Germany	61,800	18,800	2,340,000
France	9,200	4,600	550,000
United States	10,000	5,000	600,000
Total	148,100	54,600	6,610,000

In England the consumption averages 33,000 tons, in Germany 15,000.

Cattle of all Nations (1880–83).

000's omitted.

	Cows.	Horses.	Sheep.	Pigs.
United Kingdom	9,905	2,905	27,876	3,190
France	11,480	2,833	23,370	5,810
Germany	15,790	3,360	25,200	7,130
Russia	22,770	16,160	48,820	10,514
Austria	13,133	3,760	21,418	7,080
Italy	3,490	658	6,980	1,570
Spain and Portugal	3,620	659	25,217	5,323
Holland	1,462	279	898	337
Belgium	1,242	283	586	632
Denmark	1,348	352	1,720	504
Sweden and Norway	3,254	618	3,189	518
Greece	258	96	2,292	30
Roumania	3,600	600	6,180	2,310
Europe	91,352	32,563	193,766	44,948
United States	42,547	11,170	50,627	44,200
Canada	2,702	866	3,330	1,425
Australia	7,863	1,065	65,915	815
River Plate	18,390	6,150	88,440	362
Cape Colony	1,330	241	11,280	164
Algeria	1,204	350	8,788	300
The World	165,388	52,405	422,146	92,214

Production of Coffee.

Total Crop.	Tons.	In 1881.	Tons.
1832	95,000	Brazil	333,000
1844	255,000	Java	90,000
1855	321,000	Ceylon	53,000
1865	422,000	West Indies	42,000
1875	505,000	Africa, &c.	71,000
1881	589,000		
		Total	589,000

Tobacco Crop.

Exports from United States.		Product (1881).	
	Million lbs.		Tons.
1840	141	United States	210,000
1850	168	India	170,000
1860	193	Russia	75,000
1870	188	Austria	65,000
1880	217	West Indies	22,000
1883	236	Brazil, &c.	226,000
		Total	768,000

Sugar in 1882.

000's omitted.

	Tons.
Germany	606
Cuba	520
Austria	460
France	390
British Colonies	340
Russia	240
Java	190
Manilla	180
Brazil	150
French Colonies	105
Egypt, &c.	490
Total	3,671

K.

FOOD-SUPPLY.

Consumption of Luxuries.

	Ounce per Inhabitant.			Gallons per Inhabitant.		
	Tea.	Coffee.	Tobacco.	Beer.	Wine.	Spirits.
United Kingdom	72	15	23	28·6	0·4	1·1
France	1	52	29	5·1	20·1	0·9
Germany	1	83	72	19·4	2·7	1·3
Russia	7	3	26	0·8	0·4	2·2
Austria	1	35	80	6·5	7·5	0·8
Italy	1	18	22	0·7	17·6	0·3
Spain	1	4	32	0·1	13·5	0·2
Belgium and Holland	8	175	84	22·2	0·8	2·6
Denmark	8	76	61	12·6	0·3	4·3
Sweden and Norway	2	88	29	5·4	0·2	4·2
United States	21	115	59	7·2	0·6	1·5
Average	11	44	41	8·6	5·5	1·1

Consumption of Liquor in United Kingdom.

	Millions of Gallons.				Gallons per Inhabitant.			
	Beer.	Spirits.	Wine.	Equivalent in Alcohol.	Beer.	Wine.	Spirits.	Equivalent in Alcohol.
1853	720	6	26	46	26	0·22	0·96	1·67
1860	770	8	27	50	26	0·26	0·93	1·72
1871	980	16	34	64	31	0·51	1·06	2·02
1883	977	14	37	65	28	0·40	1·06	1·86

	Millions of Gallons.				Gallons per Inhabitant.			
	Beer.	Wine.	Spirits.	Equivalent in Alcohol.	Beer.	Wine.	Spirits.	Equivalent in Alcohol.
England	864	10	21	51	32	0·40	0·77	1·90
Scotland	38	2	9	7	10	0·40	2·37	1·73
Ireland	75	2	7	7	15	0·40	1·40	1·46
U. Kingdom	977	14	37	65	28	0·40	1·06	1·86

The expenditure for liquor in 1883 was 57 shillings per inhabitant in England, 58 in Scotland, and only 44 shillings in Ireland.

Butter and Cheese.

	Production, Tons, 000's omitted.			Consumption, Tons, 000's omitted.			Consumption of Butter and Cheese, lbs. per Inhabitant.
	Butter.	Cheese.	Total.	Butter.	Cheese.	Total.	
U. Kingdom	90	126	216	205	216	421	26
France	96	15	105	65	50	115	7
Germany	160	80	240	160	80	240	12
Austria	88	45	133	88	45	133	8
Italy	12	14	26	12	21	33	3
Switzerland	10	40	50	10	22	32	27
Holland	46	40	86	10	10	20	12
Scandinavia	55	20	75	40	20	60	16
United States	376	117	487	350	50	400	18
Canada	34	33	67	24	16	40	21
Total	962	530	1,485	964	530	1,494	13

The product of milch cows in Holland averages in value £15 each per annum, against £11 in England and £7 in Canada. The Camembert cows in France produce cheese to the value of £36 per head. It takes in England a gallon of milk to make a pound of cheese, a good cow giving 280 lbs. cheese per annum.

Consumption of Imports per Inhabitant (United Kingdom).

	1851–60.	1861–70.	1871–80.	1881–84.	Ratio.	
					1851–60.	1881–84.
Sugar, lbs.	31	38	58	70	100	226
Rice, ,,	6	6	11	14	100	233
Bacon, ,,	1	3	10	11	100	1,100
Butter, ,,	2	4	5	7	100	350
Cheese, ,,	1	3	5	5	100	500
Raisins, ,,	2	4	4	4	100	200
Eggs, No.	5	12	20	24	100	480
Tea, ounces	38	52	70	75	100	197
Coffee, ,,	21	17	15	14	100	67
Tobacco, ,,	18	21	23	23	100	128

L.

PRICE-LEVEL OF THE WORLD SINCE 1782.

The value of all merchandise, assuming the same quantities as in 1881–84, would have been at previous prices as follows:—

Agricultural, Millions Sterling.

Year.	Grain.	Meat.	Dairy.	Wool.	Cotton.	Sugar.	Sundries.	Total.
1782–90	1,348	342	153	272	298	96	264	2,773
1791–1800	1,803	480	202	330	327	164	347	3,653
1801–10	2,214	640	257	704	222	132	438	4,607
1811–20	2,360	706	295	560	222	159	452	4,754
1821–30	1,589	532	234	240	137	109	298	3,139
1831–40	1,490	588	220	200	122	106	286	3,012
1841–50	1,419	560	236	160	76	106	269	2,826
1851–60	1,724	628	266	145	85	100	324	3,272
1861–70	1,658	661	303	125	183	106	380	3,416
1871–80	1,547	747	333	97	101	84	384	3,293
1881–84	1,326	830	340	83	87	61	406	3,133

Manufactures, Millions Sterling.

Year.	Hardware.	Timber.	Coal.	Cottons.	Woollens.	Leather.	Sundries.	Total.
1782–90	702	235	392	926	356	196	335	3,142
1791–1800	865	325	426	1,005	395	251	370	3,637
1801–10	1,116	621	336	770	710	340	451	4,344
1811–20	1,265	560	358	770	577	330	422	4,282
1821–30	1,006	257	358	540	330	175	308	2,974
1831–40	865	299	280	502	303	196	299	2,744
1841–50	576	428	224	386	263	218	265	2,360
1851–60	525	338	241	335	245	202	271	2,157
1861–70	504	338	241	484	280	212	287	2,346
1871–80	593	301	241	346	268	188	249	2,186
1881–84	384	273	189	302	223	184	222	1,777

The prices adopted before 1840 are those of Great Britain, as those of other nations from 1782 to 1840 are not available.

APPENDIX.

Price-level of Principal Items.

Agricultural.

Year.	Grain.	Meat.	Dairy.	Wool.	Cotton.	Sugar.	Total.
1782–90	100	100	100	100	100	100	100
1791–1800	133	141	131	121	110	170	132
1801–10	165	188	167	259	75	138	166
1811–20	175	208	190	206	75	165	172
1821–30	118	157	153	90	46	113	113
1831–40	110	173	144	75	41	110	109
1841–50	105	165	155	60	26	110	102
1851–60	128	184	175	54	28	104	118
1861–70	123	194	198	46	61	110	123
1871–80	115	220	218	36	34	88	119
1881–84	98	244	222	30	29	64	113

Industrial.

Year.	Hardware.	Timber.	Coal.	Cottons.	Woollens.	Leather.	Total.
1782–90	100	100	100	100	100	100	100
1791–1800	124	138	109	107	112	128	116
1801–10	159	263	85	82	199	173	138
1811–20	181	238	91	82	161	168	136
1821–30	144	108	91	58	92	90	95
1831–40	124	127	71	54	84	100	87
1841–50	82	182	57	42	73	111	75
1851–60	75	144	61	36	68	103	69
1861–70	72	144	61	52	78	108	75
1871–80	85	128	61	37	75	96	70
1881–84	55	116	48	32	62	94	57

It appears from the above that agricultural products have risen 13 per cent., manufactures fallen 43 per cent., in price-level since 1782–90.

M.

PRICE-LISTS.

Average Value of Fifty British Imports.

		1854-60.	1861-70.	1871-80.	1881-84.	Extreme Annual Prices.	
						Highest.	Lowest.
Bacon, cwt.	s.	51	49	45	50	66 in 1869	35 in 1862
Barley, bushel	d.	37	43	50	44	61 ,, 1868	28 ,, 1865
Beef, cwt.	s.	40	38	44	51	53 ,, 1883	29 ,, 1863
Brandy, gallon	d.	112	80	95	108	156 ,, 1857	60 ,, 1866
Butter, cwt.	s.	84	104	110	103	117 ,, 1876	68 ,, 1854
Cheese, cwt.	s.	51	56	56	54	64 ,, 1866	43 ,, 1879
Cigars, lb.	s.	11	11	13	12	14 ,, 1882	6 ,, 1869
Cochineal, cwt.	£	21	16	13	9	23 ,, 1857	6 ,, 1884
Cocoa, cwt.	s.	47	55	72	74	93 ,, 1879	28 ,, 1854
Coffee, cwt.	s.	49	64	88	72	101 ,, 1874	43 ,, 1858
Copper ore, ton	£	21	15	13	10	29 .. 1856	8 ,, 1881
Cotton, cwt.	s.	61	148	66	58	271 ,, 1864	55 ,, 1879
Currants, cwt.	s.	36	21	27	27	61 ,, 1855	17 ,, 1865
Eggs, gross	d.	82	88	114	102	124 ,, 1874	65 ,, 1854
Flax, cwt.	s.	47	55	49	40	60 ,, 1866	36 ,, 1857
Flour, cwt.	s.	18	15	17	15	24 ,, 1855	13 ,, 1884
Gloves, pair	d.	20	26	25	24	28 ,, 1868	16 ,, 1855
Guano, ton	£	12	12	11	10	13 ,, 1857	9 ,, 1882
Hemp, cwt.	s.	35	35	33	32	54 ,, 1854	28 ,, 1879
Hides, cwt.	s.	66	59	82	64	89 ,, 1874	47 ,, 1854
Hops, cwt.	s.	107	93	94	144	170 ,, 1854	45 ,, 1859
Indigo, cwt.	£	31	34	27	26	38 ,, 1868	24 ,, 1884
Jute, cwt.	s.	18	19	17	14	25 ,, 1863	12 ,, 1883
Lard, cwt.	s.	58	56	47	51	73 ,, 1869	34 ,, 1879
Maize, bushel	d.	53	44	42	38	66 ,, 1855	33 ,, 1879
Molasses, cwt.	s.	13	12	9	8	18 ,, 1857	7 ,, 1884
Nitre, cwt.	s.	16	14	15	12	20 ,, 1857	11 ,, 1867
Oats, bushel	d.	35	40	46	43	57 ,, 1868	27 ,, 1864
Oil, olive, tun	£	53	58	46	40	67 ,, 1868	39 ,, 1883
Oilseed, ton	s.	170	188	182	155	202 ,, 1855	150 ,, 1884
Oranges, bushel	s.	12	11	9	8	13 ,, 1862	7 ,, 1870
Oxen, each	£	16	18	21	22	23 ,, 1878	12 ,, 1854
Pepper, cwt.	s.	46	37	48	56	70 ,, 1873	33 ,, 1864

APPENDIX.

		1854–60.	1861–70.	1871–80.	1881–84.	Extreme Annual Prices.	
						Highest.	Lowest.
Pork, cwt.	s.	44	46	40	38	62 in 1870	31 in 1879
Potatoes, cwt.	d.	42	54	66	75	81 ,, 1884	36 ,, 1854
Raisins, cwt.	s.	37	30	35	36	48 ,, 1856	25 ,, 1862
Rice, cwt.	s.	12	12	10	8	15 ,, 1867	8 ,, 1882
Rum, gallon	d.	40	28	24	22	44 ,, 1857	20 ,, 1884
Saltpetre, cwt.	s.	35	27	22	21	40 ,, 1860	18 ,, 1884
Seed-clover, cwt.	s.	65	57	48	44	77 ,, 1856	43 ,, 1882
Sheep, each	s.	41	39	45	46	49 .. 1878	31 ,, 1868
Silk, lb.	s.	18	23	19	16	27 ,, 1866	15 ,, 1884
Sugar, cwt.	s.	32	33	26	26	46 ,, 1857	21 ,, 1884
Tallow, cwt.	s.	55	45	40	38	63 ,, 1854	35 ,, 1880
Tea, lb.	d.	17	18	16	12	20 ,, 1865	12 ,, 1884
Tobacco, cwt.	s.	84	105	73	70	142 ,, 1863	62 ,, 1878
Wheat, bushel	d.	81	78	71	60	100 ,, 1854	50 ,, 1884
Wine, gallon	d.	133	67	88	84	177 ,, 1856	46 ,, 1864
Wood, load	s.	64	63	56	51	76 ,, 1854	42 ,, 1879
Wool, lb.	d.	21	18	14	12	22 ,, 1857	12 ,, 1884

Index Numbers of Fifty British Imports.

	1854–60.	1861–70.	1871–80.	1881–84.	1854.	1884.
Bacon	100	96	88	98	78	96
Barley	100	117	135	119	108	105
Beef	100	95	110	127	95	127
Brandy	100	71	84	96	89	96
Butter	100	124	131	123	81	119
Cheese	100	110	110	106	90	102
Cigars	100	100	118	109	100	100
Cochineal	100	76	62	43	105	28
Cocoa	100	117	154	160	60	165
Coffee	100	130	180	147	94	135
Copper	100	71	62	48	114	52
Cotton	100	242	108	95	88	93
Currants	100	58	75	75	61	75
Eggs	100	107	140	124	80	123
Flax	100	117	104	85	109	88
Flour	100	83	95	83	122	72
Gloves	100	130	125	120	80	110
Guano	100	100	92	83	92	75
Hemp	100	100	94	91	168	88
Hides	100	90	124	97	71	97
Hops	100	87	88	134	158	117
Indigo	100	110	88	84	77	77
Jute	100	105	95	78	127	78
Lard	100	96	81	88	90	76
Maize	100	83	80	72	113	66
Molasses	100	92	70	62	85	54
Nitre	100	87	93	75	106	62
Carry forward,	2,700	2,794	2,786	2,622	2,641	2,476

APPENDIX.

	1854–60.	1861–70.	1871–80.	1881–84.	1854.	1884.
Brght. forwd.	2,700	2,794	2,786	2,622	2,641	2,476
Oats	100	114	130	122	103	111
Oil	100	109	86	75	100	80
Oilseed	100	110	107	91	107	89
Oranges	100	92	75	67	75	60
Oxen	100	112	130	138	75	138
Pepper	100	80	104	122	102	145
Pork	100	104	91	86	102	84
Potatoes	100	128	157	180	85	192
Raisins	100	80	95	97	86	91
Rice	100	100	83	67	117	67
Rum	100	70	60	55	110	50
Saltpetre	100	77	63	60	77	52
Seeds	100	88	74	68	80	70
Sheep	100	95	110	112	72	110
Silk	100	127	105	89	83	83
Sugar	100	103	82	82	90	66
Tallow	100	81	72	68	114	68
Tea	100	105	95	70	88	70
Tobacco	100	125	88	83	89	88
Wheat	100	96	88	74	124	62
Wine	100	50	66	63	111	64
Wood	100	98	88	80	118	75
Wool	100	86	67	56	74	56
Total	5,000	5,024	4,902	4,627	4,823	4,447

Prices of Fifty British Exports.

		1854–60.	1861–70.	1871–80.	1881–84.	Extreme Annual Prices.	
						Highest.	Lowest.
Alkali, cwt.	d.	116	104	106	75	148 in 1873	73 in 1883
Bags, doz.	s.	11	10	7	5	15 ,, 1864	5 ,, 1884
Beer, barrel	s.	69	73	83	80	88 ,, 1874	66 ,, 1854
Books, cwt.	£	14	13	11	10	15 ,, 1855	9 ,, 1884
Boots, doz.	s.	60	68	62	59	72 ,, 1864	57 ,, 1881
Bottles, cwt.	d.	130	120	126	117	138 ,, 1854	111 ,, 1883
Brass, cwt.	s.	120	110	100	86	131 ,, 1857	78 ,, 1879
Butter, cwt.	s.	100	97	124	136	140 ,, 1884	92 ,, 1854
Candles, doz. lbs.	d.	150	112	92	79	224 ,, 1857	78 ,, 1882
Carpets, yard	d.	31	35	34	28	40 ,, 1867	26 ,, 1884
Cement, ton	s.	57	53	52	46	76 ,, 1856	45 ,, 1884
Cheese, cwt.	s.	81	83	83	83	88 ,, 1870	76 ,, 1854
Cloth, yard	d.	27	36	37	37	41 ,, 1884	24 ,, 1854
Coal, ton	d.	110	114	151	110	251 ,, 1873	108 ,, 1862
Copper, cwt.	s.	110	88	80	66	120 ,, 1857	59 ,, 1884
Cordage, cwt.	s.	55	53	54	50	63 ,, 1854	46 ,, 1884
Cottons, plain, 10 yds.	d.	30	42	31	26	58 ,, 1864	25 ,, 1884
,, printed, 10 yds.	d.	41	52	45	36	63 ,, 1864	36 ,, 1884
Firearms, each	s.	25	34	28	26	41 ,, 1875	18 ,, 1854

APPENDIX.

		1854-60.	1861-70.	1871-80.	1881-84.	Extreme Annual Prices.	
						Highest.	Lowest.
Fish, barrel	s.	25	27	29	30	35 in 1881	21 in 1854
Flannels, yard	d.	16	18	18	15	20 ,, 1864	14 ,, 1884
Glass, flint, cwt.	s.	64	56	54	46	73 ,, 1855	44 ,, 1881
Gunpowder, 10 lbs.	d.	74	64	61	59	77 ,, 1859	57 ,, 1868
Hats, doz.	s.	38	35	27	22	39 ,, 1865	21 ,, 1884
Horses, each	£	58	51	64	60	81 ,, 1876	35 ,, 1870
Iron, pig, ton	s.	67	57	74	52	125 ,, 1873	46 ,, 1884
,, rails, ton	s.	106	160	184	128	265 ,, 1873	114 ,, 1884
,, hoops, ton	s.	262	212	206	152	292 ,, 1873	144 ,, 1879
Jute, 10 yards	d.	53	42	34	26	60 ,, 1854	24 ,, 1884
Lead, ton	£	24	21	20	14	25 ,, 1856	13 ,, 1884
Leather, cwt.	s.	176	187	164	178	225 ,, 1866	137 ,, 1879
Linen, plain, 10 yards	d.	70	77	73	68	84 ,, 1864	66 ,, 1884
,, printed, 10 yards	d.	76	90	77	74	99 ,, 1866	65 ,, 1884
Oilseed, gallon	d.	33	35	29	24	38 ,, 1866	22 ,, 1884
Paper, cwt.	s.	88	63	56	42	96 ,, 1854	41 ,, 1884
Sailcloth, yard	d.	12	13	13	12	14 ,, 1874	11 ,, 1884
Salt, ton	s.	11	10	13	12	19 ,, 1873	9 ,, 1863
Soap, cwt.	s.	26	26	25	23	28 ,, 1869	22 ,, 1882
Silks, yard	d.	38	45	40	40	49 ,, 1867	37 ,, 1875
Spirits, gallon	d.	45	30	49	70	74 ,, 1884	29 ,, 1865
Steel, ton	£	35	32	32	15	38 ,, 1874	11 ,, 1881
Sugar, cwt.	s.	53	37	26	21	60 ,, 1857	17 ,, 1884
Tin, cwt.	s.	120	107	100	95	150 ,, 1872	66 ,, 1878
Wire, ton	£	20	20	17	14	24 ,, 1873	13 ,, 1884
Wool, lb.	d.	16	20	19	13	24 ,, 1865	11 ,, 1884
Worsted stuffs, yard	d.	10	14	11	9	15 ,, 1867	9 ,, 1879
Yarn, cotton, lb.	d.	12	20	15	12	29 ,, 1864	11 ,, 1855
,, linen, lb.	d.	13	16	16	14	18 ,, 1864	12 ,, 1855
,, woollen, lb.	d.	30	37	35	25	42 ,, 1866	23 ,, 1883
Zinc, cwt.	s.	28	22	21	14	32 ,, 1857	14 ,, 1884

Index Numbers of Fifty British Exports.

	1854-60.	1861-70.	1871-80.	1881-84.	1854.	1884.
Alkali	100	90	92	65	86	65
Bags	100	91	64	45	118	45
Beer	100	106	120	117	95	110
Books	100	93	80	72	100	64
Boots	100	113	103	98	100	100
Bottles	100	92	97	90	106	86
Brass	100	92	83	72	103	71
Butter	100	97	124	136	92	140
Candles	100	74	61	52	85	54
Carpets	100	113	110	90	94	84
Cement	100	93	91	80	98	79
Cheese	100	103	103	103	94	104
Carry forward,	1,200	1,157	1,128	1,020	1,171	1,002

APPENDIX. 183

	1854–60.	1861–70.	1871–80.	1881–84.	1854.	1884.
Brought forward,	1,200	1,157	1,128	1,020	1,171	1,002
Cloth	100	133	137	137	89	152
Coal	100	104	137	100	109	101
Copper	100	80	73	60	105	54
Cordage	100	96	98	91	114	83
Cottons, plain	100	140	103	87	93	83
,, printed	100	127	110	88	100	88
Firearms	100	136	112	104	72	104
Fish	100	108	116	120	84	100
Flannel	100	113	113	94	88	88
Glass	100	88	85	72	106	73
Gunpowder	100	85	81	80	90	77
Hats	100	92	71	58	95	55
Horses	100	88	110	104	88	100
Iron, pig	100	85	111	78	128	69
,, rails	100	96	111	77	108	69
,, hoops	100	80	78	58	85	56
Jute	100	79	64	49	113	45
Lead	100	88	83	58	96	54
Leather	100	106	93	101	95	107
Linen, plain	100	110	104	97	114	94
,, printed	100	118	101	97	100	87
Oilseed	100	106	88	73	100	67
Paper	100	71	63	48	109	46
Sailcloth	100	108	108	100	100	92
Salt	100	91	118	109	109	118
Soap	100	100	96	88	104	88
Silks	100	118	105	105	100	103
Spirits	100	67	109	155	133	165
Steel	100	91	91	43	94	57
Sugar	100	70	48	40	66	32
Tin	100	89	83	79	96	71
Wire	100	100	85	70	105	65
Wool	100	125	119	81	88	70
Worsted	100	140	110	90	110	100
Yarn, cotton	100	167	125	100	92	100
,, linen	100	123	123	108	100	108
,, woollen	100	123	117	83	80	80
Zinc	100	79	75	50	107	50
Total	5,000	5,077	4,882	4,252	4,936	4,153

Prices in United States (Gold).

		1825–30.	1831–40.	1841–50.	1851–60.	1861–70.	1871–80.	1881–83.
Beef, cwt.	s.	22	25	22	24	22	22	29
Butter, cwt.	s.	70	80	62	90	106	104	140
Cheese, cwt.	s.	33	37	28	38	46	51	65
Coal, ton	s.	33	34	25	25	26	19	18
Coffee, cwt.	s.	65	54	36	48	71	77	58
Cotton, cwt.	s.	56	58	40	50	170	65	56

APPENDIX.

		1825-30.	1831-40.	1841-50.	1851-60.	1861-70.	1871-80.	1881-83.
Flour, cwt.	s.	13	16	13	14	12	12	11
Fish, cwt.	s.	13	20	26	38	35	29	36
Hams, cwt.	s.	47	49	36	46	45	42	65
Iron, ton	s.	218	187	133	121	122	131	92
Leather, cwt.	s.	98	89	73	102	105	118	94
Maize, bushel	d.	30	40	32	40	38	28	35
Pork, cwt.	s.	30	40	25	40	40	33	35
Rice, cwt.	s.	15	17	21	19	33	32	24
Sugar, cwt.	s.	35	32	29	29	40	33	31
Tobacco, cwt.	s.	19	34	27	43	57	39	37
Wheat, bushel	d.	55	68	58	79	75	65	60
Wool, lb.	d.	14	16	14	18	19	19	20

Prices of Eggs.

Pence per Twelve Dozen.

Year.	G. Britain.	France.	Italy.	Canada.	Medium.
1851-60	80	74	53	...	69
1861-70	88	85	56	...	76
1871-80	114	95	74	79	91
1881-83	106	101	91	91	97

Prices of British Grain.

	Pence per Bushel.			Ratio.			
Year.	Wheat.	Barley.	Oats.	Wheat.	Barley.	Oats.	Average.
1841-50	80	50	33	100	100	100	100
1851	57	38	27	71	76	82	76
1852	62	42	29	77	84	88	83
1853	80	50	31	100	100	94	98
1854	108	54	42	135	108	127	123
1855	112	48	41	140	96	124	120
1856	104	62	38	130	124	115	123
1857	84	63	38	105	126	115	115
1858	66	53	38	82	106	115	101
1859	66	51	35	82	102	106	97
1860	80	56	36	100	112	109	107
1861	83	54	36	104	108	109	107
1862	83	53	35	104	106	106	105
1863	68	51	32	85	102	97	95
1864	60	45	30	75	90	91	85
1865	63	45	33	79	90	100	90
1866	75	56	36	94	112	109	105
1867	96	60	39	120	120	118	119
1868	96	64	42	120	128	127	125
1869	72	59	39	90	118	118	109
1870	70	53	35	88	106	106	100
1871	86	54	38	107	108	115	110
1872	86	56	35	107	112	106	108
1873	89	60	38	111	120	115	115

APPENDIX.

Year.	Pence per Bushel.			Ratio.			
	Wheat.	Barley.	Oats.	Wheat.	Barley.	Oats.	Average.
1874	84	67	44	105	134	133	124
1875	68	57	44	85	114	133	111
1876	69	53	39	86	106	118	103
1877	85	60	39	106	120	118	115
1878	69	60	36	86	120	109	105
1879	66	51	33	82	102	100	95
1880	66	50	35	82	100	106	96
1881	69	48	33	86	96	100	94
1882	69	47	33	86	94	100	93
1883	63	48	33	79	96	100	92
1884	54	47	30	67	94	91	84

Prices of 1854 and 1884 Compared.

		Imports				Exports	
		1854.	1884.			1854.	1884.
Bacon, cwt.	s.	40	49	Alkali, cwt.	d.	100	76
Barley, bushel	d.	40	39	Bags, doz.	s.	13	5
Beef, cwt.	s.	38	51	Beer, barrel	s.	66	76
Brandy, gallon	d.	100	108	Books, cwt.	£	14	9
Butter, cwt.	s.	68	100	Boots, doz.	s.	60	60
Cheese, cwt.	s.	46	52	Bottles, cwt.	d.	138	112
Cigars, lb.	s.	11	11	Brass, cwt.	s.	124	85
Cochineal, cwt.	£	22	6	Butter, cwt.	s.	92	140
Cocoa, cwt.	s.	28	77	Candles, doz. lbs.	d.	127	80
Coffee, cwt.	s.	46	66	Carpets, yard	d.	29	26
Copper ore, ton	£	24	11	Cement, ton	s.	56	45
Cotton, cwt.	s.	54	57	Cheese, cwt.	s.	76	84
Currants, cwt.	s.	22	27	Cloth, yard	d.	24	41
Eggs, gross	d.	65	101	Coal, ton	d.	120	111
Flax, cwt.	s.	51	41	Copper, cwt.	s.	115	59
Flour, cwt.	s.	22	13	Cordage, cwt.	s.	63	46
Gloves, pair	d.	16	22	Cottons, plain, 10 yds.	d.	28	25
Guano, ton	£	11	9	,, printed, ,,	d.	41	36
Hemp, cwt.	s.	59	31	Firearms, each	s.	18	26
Hides, cwt.	s.	47	64	Fish, barrel	s.	21	25
Hops, cwt.	s.	170	126	Flannel, yard	d.	14	14
Indigo, cwt.	£	24	24	Glass, cwt.	s.	68	47
Jute, cwt.	s.	23	14	Gunpowder, 10 lbs.	d.	67	58
Lard, cwt.	s.	52	44	Hats, doz.	s.	36	21
Maize, bushel	d.	60	35	Horses, each	£	51	58
Molasses, cwt.	s.	11	7	Iron, pig, ton	s.	85	46
Nitre, cwt.	s.	17	10	,, rails, ton	s.	180	114
Oats, bushel	d.	36	39	,, hoops, ton	s.	226	146
Oil, tun	£	53	42	Jute, 10 yards	d.	60	24
Oilseed, ton	s.	183	151	Lead, ton	£	23	13
Oranges, bushel	s.	9	7	Leather, cwt.	s.	167	189
Oxen, each	£	12	22	Linen, plain, 10 yards	d.	80	66
Pepper, cwt.	s.	47	66	,, printed ,,	d.	76	65

186   APPENDIX.

	Imports. 1854.	Imports. 1884.			Exports. 1854.	Exports. 1884.
Pork, cwt. . . . *s.*	45	37	Oilseed, gallon .	*d.*	33	22
Potatoes, cwt. . . *d.*	36	81	Paper, cwt. . .	*s.*	96	41
Raisins, cwt. . . *s.*	32	34	Sailcloth, yard .	*d.*	12	11
Rice, cwt. . . . *s.*	14	8	Salt, ton . .	*s.*	12	13
Rum, gallon . . *d.*	44	20	Silks, yard . .	*d.*	38	39
Saltpetre, cwt. . . *s.*	27	18	Soap, cwt. . .	*s.*	27	23
Seeds, cwt. . . . *s.*	52	45	Spirits, gallon .	*d.*	60	74
Sheep, each . . . *s.*	30	45	Steel, ton . .	£	33	20
Silk, lb. . . . *s.*	15	15	Sugar, cwt. . .	*s.*	35	17
Sugar, cwt. . . *s.*	29	21	Tin, cwt. . .	*s.*	116	85
Tallow, cwt. . . *s.*	63	38	Wire, ton . .	£	21	13
Tea, lb. . . . *d.*	15	12	Wool, lb. . .	*d.*	14	11
Tobacco, cwt. . . *s.*	74	73	Worsted, yard .	*d.*	11	10
Wheat, bushel . . *d.*	100	50	Yarn, cotton, lb.	*d.*	11	12
Wine, gallon . . *d.*	148	85	,, linen, lb. .	*d.*	13	14
Wood, load . . . *s.*	76	48	,, woollen, lb.	*d.*	24	24
Wool, lb. . . . *d.*	16	12	Zinc, cwt. . .	*s.*	30	14

Prices in England for 700 Years

(According to Weight of Silver).

	1201-1300	1301-1400	1401-1500	1501-1600	1601-1700	1701-1800	1801-80
Ox . . *s.*	43	45	42	40	106	170	340
Horse . . *s.*	...	80	84	80	106	275	600
Sheep . . *s.*	3	4	4	4	8	19	30
Pig . . *s.*	6	9	6	6	9	23	30
Wheat, bush. *d.*	...	24	23	32	70	80	85
Wine, gal. . *s.*	3	3	2	4	6	17	20
Beer, gal. . *d.*	3	5	4	4	4	8	16
Goose . . *d.*	9	12	12	11	12	25	50
Hen . . *d.*	3	6	6	5	9	12	18
Beef, cwt. . *s.*	7	14	12	9	28	43	70
Butter, cwt. . *s.*	...	37	28	28	37	47	112
Eggs, doz. . *d.*	3	6	6	4	4	8	12

Prices in France since A.D. 1400.

	1401-1500.	1501-1600.	1601-1700.	1701-90.	1820-30.	1850-60.	1870-80.
Wine, gal. *d.*	4	8	12	15	18	25	22
Meat, lb. *d.*	...	2	3	3	4	6	8
Eggs, doz. *d.*	2	2	3	3	4	6	9
Sugar, lb. *d.*	...	...	6	8	11	8	5
Butter, lb. *d.*	...	3	4	6	7	10	14
Wheat, bsh. *d.*	18	19	33	44	66	78	80

APPENDIX.

Prices of Wheat in England and France
(Pence per Bushel, according to Weight of Silver).

Year.	England.	France.	Year.	England.	France.
1301–1400	25	17	1651–1700	70	24
1401–1500	19	18	1701–50	59	38
1501–50	30	15	1751–1800	100	54
1551–1600	33	23	1801–50	91	69
1601–50	63	41	1851–80	76	77

In England the extreme prices have been per bushel as follows :—

Highest.		Lowest.	
Year.	Pence.	Year.	Pence.
1316	72	1392	14
1434	96	1454	6
1597	96	1509	9
1648	120	1687	36
1796	124	1744	34
1812	170	1884	50

Price-Levels in England.

	1301–1400	1401–1500	1501–1600	1601–1700	1701–1800	1801–50	1880–84
Cattle	100	95	80	160	246	350	500
Beer	100	80	80	80	160	280	350
Butter	100	75	75	100	125	250	350
Grain	100	95	133	270	330	350	240
Horses	100	105	100	132	346	700	800
Wine	100	70	130	200	500	600	700
Eggs	100	100	70	70	135	160	270
Meat	100	85	65	200	300	400	550
Total	800	705	733	1,212	2,142	3,090	3,760

INDEX NUMBERS.
'*Professor Jevons's Table of Forty Articles.*

Years.	Metals.	Fibre.	Grain.	Col. Products.	General Average.
1782	100	100	100	100	100
1783–90	95	102	109	88	91
1791–1800	116	119	135	86	112
1801–10	150	157	170	71	133
1811–20	124	134	166	72	115
1821–30	102	97	135	56	88
1831–40	91	96	134	53	83
1841–50	88	76	127	42	73
1851–60	97	84	132	39	79
1861–69	93	105	128	40	77

Another Table of Professor Jevons.

Year.	Number.	Year.	Number.	Year.	Number.
1789	100	1819	131	1849	75
1799	151	1829	93	1859	90
1809	184	1839	108	1869	89

Table of Fifty Articles (Jevons).

Year.	Number.	Year.	Number.	Year.	Number.
1846	100	1854	115	1862	108
1847	106	1855	112	1863	107
1848	89	1856	117	1864	106
1849	85	1857	123	1865	105
1850	87	1858	108	1866	111
1851	87	1859	110	1867	102
1852	89	1860	112	1868	104
1853	106	1861	110	1869	103

Soetbeer's Price-Level.

Year.	Number.	Year.	Number.	Year.	Number.
1847-50	100	1871	128	1877	131
1851-55	114	1872	137	1878	125
1856-60	125	1873	141	1879	120
1861-65	127	1874	140	1880	126
1866-70	125	1875	133	1881	124
1871-80	131	1876	133	1882	124

Table from the "Economist" (Twenty-two Articles).

Year.	Number.	Year.	Number.	Year.	Number.
1845-50	100	1872	129	1878	115
1857	136	1873	134	1879	100
1866	162	1874	131	1880	115
1867	137	1875	126	1881	108
1870	122	1876	123	1882	111
1871	118	1877	124	1883	107

N.

VARIOUS WRITERS ON PRICES.

The continued influx from the American mines in the sixteenth century was quite inadequate to produce any progressive effects on the general price of commodities in Europe.—*Adam Smith.*

It is a lamentable sign of ignorance that the fall in prices (1826) is supposed to be connected with metallic currency.—*N. Senior.*

Steadiness in value depends upon the permanence of the intrinsic causes of value.—*Ibid.*

It has been customary to ascribe the fall in prices since 1815 to the diminished supply of bullion from the mines (1830), but I doubt if this circumstance has had any influence in that way.—*M'Culloch.*

It is not wages that affect prices, but an increase or diminution of the labour necessary to produce the commodity. A rise of wages has no effect on the price of commodities.—*Ibid.*

Causes affecting the cost of production and the supply and demand for each commodity account for the variation of prices.—*Tooke.*

The quantity of precious metals may remain constant and the trade in a country be doubled, but the prices of commodities will not vary in the least degree.—*Ibid.*

It is a fallacy to suppose that the range of prices depends on the quantity of money. The range of general prices has not been materially influenced by the gold-fields of California and Australia.—*Ibid.*

An advance in the price of provisions is not accompanied by a corresponding rise in the wages of labour.—*Ibid.*

The price of grain suffers extreme depression more than other things, because the average quantity is sufficient for all, and anything beyond that causes inconvenient accumulation. An excess of crop, however, does not depress price in the same degree that a deficient crop drives it up.—*Tooke.*

Wages and prices do not rise together. In the sixteenth century prices in England fell, while the wages of labour rose.—*Ibid.*

The wages of a day labourer are the best criterion of value.—*Ibid.*

Europe was on the verge of bankruptcy in 1792, prices having been unduly inflated by speculators, such was the abundance of unemployed capital looking for investment.—*Ibid.*

Prices of agricultural products rose so high in 1795 that the farmers realised enormous gains and landlords raised their rents; but the distress among the working-class was so severe that the members of both Houses of Parliament signed a covenant to reduce the consumption of bread in their households by one-third.—*Ibid.*

In the early years of the gold discoveries I arrived at an opinion, then considered heretical, that the effect of the discoveries would not be to augment general prices, and this is now recognised as an orthodox conclusion.—*Newmarch.*

Whatever causes augment the real wealth and resources of the world serve not only to stimulate trade, but also to keep down prices. The object of all scientific methods applied to commerce and the arts is cheapness, and the tendency of prices is towards decline, by reason of the enlarging facilities and power of production.—*Ibid.*

INDEX.

Accumulation of wealth, 110, 113.
Affghan-Russo question, 152.
Africa, South. *See* Cape Colony.
Agricultural industry, 78, 84, 171.
—— machinery, 144, 146.
—— products, 123, 131, 171.
—— values, 177.
—— wages, 125, 132.
Agriculture, capital in, 84.
—— men engaged in, 115.
Alabama claims, 149.
Alcohol. *See* Liquor.
Alexandria bombarded, 151.
Alfonso, king of Spain, 150.
Algeria, cattle, 173.
—— ironstone, 73.
—— railways, 47.
—— wine-growing, 172.
Alkali, price of, 181.
Amadeo, king of Spain, 149.
America, North. *See* United States.
America, Spanish, commerce, 35, 164.
—— debts, 163.
—— emigration to, 101.
—— mining industry, 76.
—— population, 96.
—— railways, 47.
—— silver product, 13.
—— telegraphs, 50.
Arabi Pasha, 152.
Argentine Republic, agriculture, 84.
—— earnings, 112.
—— finances, 162.

Argentine Republic, import dues, 37.
—— wealth, 110.
—— wine-growing, 172.
—— *See* River Plate.
Armies and navies, 29, 115.
Artisans' wages, 125.
Assets in bankruptcy, 24.
Australia, agriculture, 80, 84, 172.
—— banking capital, 160.
—— books and journals, 69.
—— cattle, 173.
—— coinage, 16, 157.
—— commerce, 36, 103, 142, 164.
—— current of gold, 15, 157.
—— death-rate and sickness, 99.
—— debt, 30, 104, 151.
—— earnings and wealth, 30, 110, 112.
—— emigration to, 102.
—— finances, 26, 104.
—— gold product, 13, 71, 159.
—— import duties, 37.
—— meat frozen from, 151.
—— mining industry, 76.
—— population, 96, 103.
—— railways, 47, 167.
—— steamers, first, 145.
—— telegraphs, 50.
—— wages in, 126.
—— wealth and earnings, 30, 110, 112.
—— wine-growing, 172.
—— wool-clip, 60.

INDEX.

Austria, agriculture, 80, 84, 171.
—— banking, 19, 21, 160.
—— books and paper, 69.
—— capital, new, 22.
—— cattle, 173.
—— coinage, 16, 157.
—— commerce, 35, 164.
—— cost of industry, 55.
—— death-rate and sickness, 99.
—— debt and finances, 26, 30.
—— earnings and wealth, 30, 110, 112.
—— food-supply, 86, 92.
—— import duties, 37.
—— iron and steel, 64.
—— living, cost of, 113.
—— manufactures, textile, 168.
—— military expenditure, 28.
—— mining industry, 73, 76.
—— population, 96.
—— railways, 47, 167.
—— savings banks, 23.
—— steam power, 53.
—— sugar production, 174.
—— summary of industries, 115.
—— telegraphs, 50.
—— timber industry, 67.
—— tobacco cultivation, 174.
—— wages, 125, 132.

BACON, consumption of, in Great Britain, 176.
—— export from United States, 91.
—— price of, 179, 185.
Bags, empty, price of, 181.
Bailiff's wages, 131.
Balance of trade, 36, 164.
Ballast entries in Great Britain, 45.
Bank Act suspended, 3, 146.
Bank of England, 21.
Banks of Europe, 21.
Banking capital, 23, 160.
Bankruptcy returns, 24.
Barley crop of world, 80.
—— cultivation in Gt. Britain, 172.
—— price of, 179, 184.

Beef. *See* Meat.
—— price of, 179, 183, 185, 186.
Beer, consumption, 175.
—— price, 181, 186.
—— value, 117.
Beetle, Colorado, 150.
Beetroot. *See* Sugar.
Belgium, agriculture, 80, 84, 171.
—— banking, 19, 21, 160.
—— books and paper, 69.
—— cattle, 173.
—— coinage, 16, 157.
—— commerce, 35, 142, 164.
—— cost of industry, 55.
—— cost of living, 113.
—— debt and taxes, 30, 163.
—— finances, 26, 162.
—— food-supply, 86, 92, 175.
—— iron and steel, 64.
—— manufactures, textile, 168.
—— mining, 73, 76.
—— population, 96.
—— price-level, 6, 155.
—— railways, 47, 167.
—— shipping entries, 166.
—— steam-power, 53.
—— wages, 125, 132.
—— wealth and earnings, 30, 110.
Berlin clearing-house, 160.
—— crisis, 149.
Bessemer steel, 64, 119, 148.
Blacksmiths' wages, 125, 131.
Bland silver law, 14, 151.
Books and paper, 68, 122.
—— price of, 181.
Boots and shoes, 56, 181.
Bottles, price of, 181.
Bounties, French, 44.
Brandy, price of, 179, 185.
Brass, price of, 181.
Brazil, coffee crop, 173.
—— finances, 162.
—— forests, 67.
—— import dues, 37.
—— sugar crop, 174.
—— tobacco crop, 174.

INDEX.

Brazil, trade with Great Britain, 104.
Bread, its nutritive value, 88.
Breadwinners to population, 99.
Bridges and roads, 30.
Buenos Ayres, building at, 109.
Building in cities, 109.
Bullion in banks, 20, 21.
—— sent over sea, 15, 157.
—— *See* Gold and Silver.
Butter, product and consumption, 176.
—— price of, 120, 130, 179, 183, 186.

CAB FARE in New York, 137.
Cabin passengers, ratio of, 102.
Cables, telegraph, 50.
Camembert cheese, 176.
Canada, agriculture, 80, 171.
—— banking, 160.
—— bankruptcy returns, 24.
—— books and paper, 69.
—— cattle, 173.
—— commerce, 36, 142, 164.
—— debt and revenue, 30.
—— Dominion formed, 148.
—— emigration to, 102.
—— finances, 26, 162.
—— import dues, 37.
—— population, 96.
—— railways, 47, 167.
—— telegraphs, 50.
—— timber, 67.
—— treaty with United States, 145.
—— wages, 133.
—— wealth and earnings, 30, 110.
Canal, Panama, 151.
—— Suez, 44, 165.
Candles, price of, 181.
Cape Colony, cattle, 173.
—————— commerce, 103.
—————— finances, 104, 163.
—————— population, 103.
—————— railways, 47.
—————— telegraphs, 50.

Cape Colony, wine-growing, 172.
—————— wool, 60.
Capital, abundance of, 4, 22.
—— agricultural, 84.
—— banking, 23, 160.
—— competition of, 127.
Carlist war, 150.
Carpenters' wages, 125, 131.
Carpets, price of, 120, 181.
Carrying-trade, 35, 41, 49.
Cattle of all nations, 83, 173.
Cattle-plague in England, 148.
Causes affecting prices, 134.
Cement, price of, 181.
Ceylon, trade, &c., 103, 173.
Channel tunnel, 152.
Charcoal for iron, 73.
Cheese, price of, 9, 120, 179, 181, 183.
—— production of, 176.
Chicago fire, 149.
Chili, copper, 74.
—— import dues, 37.
—— trade with, 104.
—— wine-growing, 172.
China, commerce, 36, 142.
—— silk, 168.
—— war in, 146.
Chronicle of events, 144.
Cigars, price of, 179, 185.
City improvements, 30.
Clearing-House returns, 21, 160.
Clothing, expenditure for, 113.
Cloth, price of, 181.
Coal, exports, 35, 73.
—— price, 120, 130, 181, 183.
—— production, 72.
—— used for iron, 73, 136.
—— value, 122, 177.
Coal-fields, alarm about, 149.
Cobden treaty, 4, 147.
Cochineal, price of, 179, 185.
Cocoa, price of, 179, 185.
Coffee, consumption, 175, 176.
—— price, 121, 130, 179, 183.
—— production, 94, 173.

INDEX.

Coffee, value, 122.
Coinage, gold and silver, 13, 157.
—— new German, 150.
Colonies, agriculture, 79.
—— commerce, 38, 103.
—— emigration to, 101.
—— finances, 104.
—— population, 103.
—— shipping, 43, 166.
—— sugar-crop, 174.
Commerce, British, 33, 142.
—— of all nations, 33.
Consols, British, 24.
Co-operative societies, 170.
Copper industry, 74.
—— price, 130, 179, 181, 185.
Cordage, price of, 181, 185.
Cotton, consumption, 58, 62.
—— crop, 59.
—— goods, price of, 181, 185.
—— manufactures, 59, 168.
—— raw, price of, 119, 130, 179, 183.
—— transport, 35.
Cotton-spinner's wages, 125.
Cowper's regenerator, 73.
Cows. See Cattle.
Crimean war, 145.
—— loans, 146.
Crises, commercial, 3, 146, 148.
Crops, value, 84.
Cuba, sugar, 174.
Currants, price of, 179, 185.
Cyprus annexed, 151.
Czar assassinated, 151.

Dairy-products, 93, 120, 177.
Dakota grain-farms, 81.
Death-rate of nations, 99.
Debts, public, 30, 105, 163.
—— converted, 151.
Decrease of rural population, 98.
Delusions regarding prices, 137.
Denmark, agriculture, 84.
—— cattle, 173.
—— finances, 162.

Denmark, food-supply, 87, 175.
—— military, 28.
—— population, 96.
—— railways, 47, 167.
—— wealth and earnings, 110.
—— See Scandinavia.
Deposits in banks, 20, 160.
—— savings-banks, 4, 23, 160.
Diamond-fields, product, 75, 149.
Discount, rates of, 19.
Dues, import, of nations, 37.

Earnings of nations, 30, 107, 112.
Economist price-level, 7, 188.
Eggs, consumption, 93, 176.
—— price, 120, 138, 179, 184, 186.
Egypt, commerce, 36, 164.
—— finances, 162.
—— Goschen's mission, 150.
—— railways, 47.
—— sugar-crop, 174.
Electric light, 150.
Electro-plate, its effect, 11.
Elgin treaty, 145.
Emigrant, his value, 103.
Emigrants, remittances by, 102.
—— in United States, 102.
Emigration, tide of, 3, 101.
—— effects of, 136.
Employés number of, 115.
Employer's share of profits, 127.
Energy contained in food, 87.
—— cost of, 55.
—— foot-tons of, 53, 88.
—— increase of, 56.
Engines. See Steam-power.
England, agriculture, 172.
—— bank of, 20.
—— emigration from, 102.
—— population, 96.
—— prices for 700 years, 186.
—— wealth, 111.
—— See Great Britain.
Entries, tonnage of, 166.
Europe, agriculture, 79, 84, 171.
—— banking, 23, 160.

INDEX. 195

Europe, books and paper, 69.
—— capital invested, 22.
—— cattle, 173.
—— coinage, 16, 157.
—— commerce, 35, 164.
—— cost of industry, 55.
—— death-rate, 99.
—— debt and taxes, 30, 163.
—— discount rates, 19.
—— earnings and wealth, 30, 110.
—— emigration from, 101.
—— euergy, amount of, 53.
—— entries, shipping, 43.
—— finances, 26, 162.
—— import dues, 37.
—— leather trade, 68.
—— living, cost of, 113.
—— manufactures, 64.
—— merchandise, ton of, 45.
—— military statistics, 28.
—— population, 96.
—— railways, 47, 167.
—— railway tariffs, 49.
—— savings-banks, 23, 160.
—— sickness, days of, 99.
—— steam-power, 52.
—— summary, industrial, 115.
—— taxes, 30, 37.
—— telegraphs, 50.
—— timber, 67.
—— vineyards, 172.
—— wages, 125, 132.
—— wealth, 30, 110.
—— wool-clip, 60.
Events, chronicle of, 144.
Exhibitions, international, 144, 148, 150.
Expenditure. *See* Finances.
Exports. *See* Commerce.

FAILURES. *See* Bankruptcy.
Famine in Bengal, 150.
Farms. *See* Agriculture.
Fibre, consumption of, 58, 62.
Finances of nations, 26, 162.
Firearms, price of, 181.

Fish, price of, 182, 184.
Fisheries question, 145.
Flannel, price of, 120, 182.
Flax, consumption, 62, 169.
—— cultivation, 61, 171.
—— price, 130, 179, 185.
Flour, price of, 179, 184.
Food, consumption, 86, 92, 175.
—— cost of, 93.
—— of Great Britain, 143.
Forests of world, 67.
Fortifications, Palmerston's, 147.
France, agriculture, 80, 84, 171.
—— banking, 21, 160.
—— bankruptcy, 24.
—— capital invested, 22.
—— cattle, 173.
—— coinage, 16, 157.
—— commerce, 35, 164.
—— cost of industry, 55.
—— death-rate, 99.
—— debt, 30, 163.
—— discounts, 19.
—— earnings, 30, 112.
—— emigration from, 101.
—— energy, 53.
—— finances, 26, 162.
—— food-supply, 86, 92, 175.
—— gold and silver, 15, 157.
—— import dues, 37.
—— index numbers, 9.
—— living, cost of, 113.
—— manufactures, 59, 65, 168.
—— military, 28.
—— mining, 73, 76.
—— population, 96.
—— price-level, 6, 155.
—— prices for 500 years, 186.
—— railways, 47, 167.
—— savings-banks, 23.
—— shipping, 43, 166.
—— steam-power, 53.
—— sugar, 174.
—— summary, industrial, 115
—— telegraphs, 50.
—— timber, 67.

France, trade with G. Britain, 142.
—— vineyards, 172.
—— wages, 125, 132.
—— wealth, 30, 110.
—— wine, 121.
Franco-German war, cost of, 30.
Free-trade, effects of, 4.
Freight, sea and land, 41, 45, 48.
Frozen meat, Australian, 151.
Fruit, price of, 135.

GEESE, price of, 186.
German gold-money, 13, 150.
Germany, agriculture, 80, 84, 171.
—— banking, 21, 160.
—— books, 69.
—— capital invested, 22.
—— cattle, 173.
—— coinage, 16, 157.
—— commerce, 35, 164.
—— cost of industry, 55.
—— death-rate, 99.
—— debt, 30, 163.
—— discounts, 19.
—— earnings, 30, 112.
—— emigration from, 101.
—— energy, 53.
—— finances, 26, 162.
—— food-supply, 86, 92, 175.
—— import dues, 37.
—— living, cost of, 113.
—— manufactures, 59, 64, 168.
—— military, 28.
—— mining, 73, 76.
—— population, 96.
—— railways, 47, 167.
—— savings-banks, 23.
—— shipping, 43, 166.
—— steam-power, 53.
—— sugar, 174.
—— summary, industrial, 115.
—— telegraphs, 50.
—— timber, 67.
—— trade with Great Britain, 142.
—— vineyards, 172.
—— wages, 125, 132.

Germany, wealth, 30, 110.
Glasgow, building in, 109.
Glass, price of, 182.
Gloves, price of, 179, 185.
Gold, amount of, 11, 158.
—— coin in use, 16, 157.
—— consumption of, 13, 158.
—— diggers, 72.
—— exports and imports, 15.
—— production, 13, 71, 159.
Goods traffic, 49, 51.
Goschen in Egypt, 150.
Grain consumption, 92.
—— crops of world, 79.
—— exports, 35.
—— in United States, 171.
—— in Great Britain, prices, 184.
—— sum spent for, 86.
—— value of, 122, 177.
—— *See* Wheat, Barley, &c.
Grease in wool, 60.
Great Britain, agriculture, 80, 84, 172.
—— banking, 20, 23, 160.
—— bankruptcy returns, 24.
—— books and paper, 69.
—— capital invested, 22.
—— cattle, 83, 173.
—— coinage, 16, 157.
—— commerce, 34, 38, 142, 164.
—— cost of industry, 55.
—— cotton industry, 59, 168.
—— death-rate, 99.
—— debt, 30, 163.
—— discounts, 19.
—— earnings, 30, 112.
—— emigration, 102.
—— energy, 53.
—— finances, 26, 162.
—— food-supply, 86, 92, 175.
—— gold and silver, 15, 157.
—— import dues, 37, 164.
—— index numbers, 180, 182, 187.
—— iron and steel, 64.
—— jute industry, 62.

INDEX.

Great Britain, leather, 68.
—— liquor, 175.
—— living, cost of, 113.
—— manufactures, 59, 64, 104, 168.
—— military, 28.
—— mining, 73, 76.
—— population, 96.
—— price-levels, 131, 154.
—— price-lists, 179, 184, 187.
—— railways, 47, 50, 167.
—— savings-banks, 23, 161.
—— shipping, 43, 166.
—— shipbuilding, 66.
—— sickness, 99.
—— silver, 15, 157.
—— silver plate, 12.
—— steam-power, 52.
—— summary, industrial, 115.
—— taxation, 30, 162.
—— telegraphs, 50.
—— timber, 67.
—— wages, 125, 132.
—— wealth, 30, 110.
—— See England, Scotland, Ireland.
Greece, agriculture, 84.
—— cattle, 173.
—— commerce, 36.
—— debt, 163.
—— earnings, 112.
—— population, 96.
—— wealth, 110.
Guano, price of, 179, 185.
Gunpowder, price of, 182.

Hams, price of, 184.
Hand, work done by, 53.
Hardware manufactures, 64, 119, 122.
—— value of, 177.
Hats, price of, 182.
Hemp industry, 62, 169.
—— price of, 179, 185.
Hens, price of, 186.
Hicks's army, 152.

Hides, price of, 179, 185.
Holland, agriculture, 80, 84, 171.
—— books and paper, 69.
—— commerce, 35, 164.
—— cost of industry, 55.
—— death-rate, 99.
—— debt, 30, 163.
—— discounts, 19.
—— earnings, 30, 112.
—— energy, 53.
—— finances, 162.
—— food-supply, 86, 92, 175.
—— liquor, 175.
—— living, cost of, 113.
—— military, 28.
—— population, 96.
—— railways, 47, 167.
—— shipping, 166.
—— steam-power, 53.
—— telegraphs, 50.
—— wages, 125.
—— wealth, 30, 110.
Hops, cultivation of, 173.
—— price of, 179, 185.
Horses, number of, 83.
—— price of, 182, 186.
—— taken for armies, 28.
—— work done by, 53.
Horse-power. See Steam-power and Energy.
Houses, value of, 109.
House rent, rise of, 132, 142.
Hungary. See Austria.
Hussey's reaper, 145.

Import dues, 37.
Imports of Great Britain, 142, 153.
—— and exports compared, 36, 164.
—— See Commerce.
Income-tax, British, 142, 147.
Index-numbers, 78, 143, 180, 182.
Indigo, price of, 179, 185.
India, capital invested, 22.
—— coinage, 16.
—— commerce, 35, 164.

INDEX.

India, cotton, 59.
—— debt, 163.
—— finances, 26, 162.
—— import dues, 37.
—— jute, 62.
—— manufactures, 168.
—— mutiny in, 146.
—— railways, 47, 167.
—— silver, 14.
—— telegraphs, 50.
—— tobacco, 174.
—— trade with Great Britain, 142.
—— wheat-growing, 80.
Indies. *See* West Indies.
Industries, summary of, 115, 117.
Inventions, effect of, 64, 136, 148.
Ireland, agriculture, 172.
—— emigration, 102.
—— incidence of taxes, 111.
—— population, 96.
—— wealth, 111.
—— *See* Great Britain.
Iron, coal used for, 73.
—— exports of, 35.
—— price of, 119, 130, 182, 184.
—— production, 64.
Ironclads, cost of, 66.
—— first used, 147.
—— largest afloat, 66.
Ironstone, yield of, 73.
Ismail Pacha, 151.
Issue of banks, 20.
Italy, agriculture, 80, 84, 171.
—— banking, 19, 160.
—— books and paper, 69.
—— capital invested, 22.
—— cattle, 173.
—— coinage, 16, 157.
—— commerce, 35, 164.
—— cost of industry, 55.
—— death-rate, 99.
—— debt, 30, 163.
—— earnings, 30, 112.
—— emigration, 101.
—— energy, 53.
—— finances, 26, 162.

Italy, food-supply, 86, 92, 175.
—— import dues, 37.
—— liquor, 175.
—— living, cost of, 113.
—— manufactures, 168.
—— military, 28.
—— mining, 74, 76.
—— population, 96.
—— price-level, 6, 155.
—— railways, 47, 167.
—— shipping, 43, 166.
—— silk, 169.
—— steam-power, 53.
—— summary, industrial, 115.
—— telegraphs, 50.
—— timber, 67.
—— vineyards, 172.
—— wages, 125, 132.
—— wealth, 30, 110.
—— wine, price of, 121.

Jablochkoff's light, 150.
Japan, copper, 74.
—— finances, 162.
—— railway, 149.
—— silk, 169.
Java, coffee, 173.
—— commerce, 36, 164.
—— railways, 47.
—— sugar, 174.
—— tin, 75.
Jevons on coin, 14.
—— price-levels, 7, 187.
Jews, persecution of, 151.
Joint-stock companies, 3, 148.
Jute industry, 61.
—— price of, 179, 182, 185.

Kerosene. *See* Petroleum.

Labour, cost of, 55.
—— daily, of nations, 53.
—— economy of, 56, 81, 135.
—— steam, done by, 53.
Labourers' wages, 132.
—— *See* Workmen.

INDEX. 199

Lake traffic, United States, 165.
Land, value of, 84, 108.
Lard, price of, 179, 185.
Laspeyre's price-level, 7.
Lead industry, 74, 130.
—— price of, 182.
Leather industry, 68, 122, 177.
—— price of, 182, 184.
Legacy returns, 142.
Light-dues in Holland, 150.
Limited Liability Act, 146.
Linen exports, 61.
—— manufactures, 63, 169.
—— price of, 182.
—— value of, 122.
Liquor consumption, 92, 175.
—— sum spent in, 86, 89.
Liverpool, house-building in, 109.
Living, cost of, 113.
Loans, foreign, 22, 146, 149.
—— fraudulent, 150.
Locomotives, steam-power of, 52.
London Clearing-House, 21, 160.
—— house-building, 109.
Loss of gold and silver, 14.
Luxuries, consumption of, 175.

MACHINERY, agricultural, 81, 144, 146.
—— industrial, 56.
Maize, price of, 179, 184.
Manchester Clearing-House, 160.
Manilla sugar-crop, 174.
Manufactures, consumers of British, 104.
—— cotton, 59, 63, 168.
—— hardware, 64.
—— jute, 61.
—— linen, 61, 169.
—— men engaged in, 115.
—— silk, 62, 168.
—— textile, 58, 63, 168.
—— value of, 123, 131.
—— woollen, 60, 63, 170.
Masons' wages, 125, 131.
Mauritius, statistics of, 103.

M'Culloch on prices, 189.
—— silver, 12.
Meat, consumption of, 90, 92, 143.
—— exports of, 35, 91.
—— in Australia, 91, 151.
—— France, 89.
—— Great Britain, 90.
—— River Plate, 91.
—— United States, 91.
—— price of, 118, 130.
—— sum spent for, 86.
—— value of, 122, 177.
—— *See* Beef.
Melbourne Clearing-House, 160.
Merchandise, weight and value, 34, 45.
Mercury, product and consumption, 75.
Messages, telegraphic, 50.
Mexico, expedition to, 147.
—— trade with Great Britain, 104.
—— wealth of, 110.
Military expenditure, 28, 162.
Mining industry, 71, 76, 115.
Mississippi steamboat traffic, 165.
Missouri lead-mines, 74.
Molasses, price of, 179, 185.
Money market, 19, 160.
Mont Cenis tunnel, 149.
Montevideo house-building, 109.
Mutton. *See* Meat.

NAVIGATION laws, petition for, 145.
Neilson's "hot-blast," 73.
New York Clearing-House, 160.
—— house-building, 109.
Newmarch's opinions, 1, 135, 189.
Nice, annexation of, 147.
Nitre, price of, 179, 185.
Norway, agriculture, 84.
—— earnings, 112.
—— population, 96.
—— wealth, 110.
—— *See* Sweden, Scandinavia.
Nugget, the largest, 72.

OATS in Great Britain, 172.
—— crop of all nations, 80.
—— price of, 179, 184.
Ocean telegraph cables, 50.
Ohio river traffic, 165.
Oil, price of, 179, 185.
Oilseed, price of, 179, 182, 185.
Operatives. *See* Workmen.
Oranges, price of, 179, 185.
Overend Gurney crisis, 3, 148.
Oxen, price of, 179, 185.

PALMERSTON'S fortifications, 147.
Paper consumption, 69.
—— duties abolished, 147.
—— price of, 182.
Paris Clearing-House, 160.
—— house-building, 109.
Passengers, cabin and steerage, 102.
—— tariff on railways, 49.
Peasant proprietors, 108.
Pekin, capture of, 147.
Pepper, price of, 179.
Peru, British exports to, 104.
Petroleum, yield and price, 75.
Phylloxera, ravages of, 94.
Pigs, price of, 186.
—— *See* Cattle.
Plate, quantity stamped, 158.
—— *See* River Plate.
Plevna, capture of, 150.
Plimsoll Shipping Act, 150.
Plough. *See* Steam-plough.
Plumbers' wages, 125, 131.
Population, breadwinners to, 99.
—— increase, rate of, 97.
—— rural, declining, 98.
Pork, price of, 180, 184, 186.
—— *See* Meat.
Portugal, agriculture, 84, 172.
—— cost of industry, 55.
—— debt, 163.
—— earnings, 112.
—— energy, 53.
—— finances, 162.

Portugal, land, value of, 110.
—— military, 28.
—— population, 96.
—— railways, 47, 167.
—— steam-power, 53.
—— vineyards, 172.
—— wealth, 110.
Potatoes, area under, 171.
—— in Great Britain, 172.
—— price of, 121, 180, 186.
—— value of, 122.
Precious metals. *See* Gold, Silver.
Price-levels, British, 154.
—— European, 6, 155.
—— of the world, 177.
—— by various writers, 7, 188.
—— of agriculture, 177.
—— of manufactures, 177.
—— of food, 93.
Price of silver, 12.
Prices affected by duties, 40.
—— —— emigration, 101.
—— —— energy, 56.
—— —— military outlay, 29.
—— —— money-market, 19.
—— —— population, 96.
—— —— railways, 48, 51.
—— —— raw material, 58, 74.
—— —— shipping, 41.
—— —— steam-power, 52.
—— —— taxation, 26.
—— —— telegraphs, 50.
Prices, American, sixty years, 183.
—— British, thirty years, 179.
—— British, 100 years, 130.
—— English, 700 years, 186.
—— French, 500 years, 186.
—— general survey of, 117, 130.
Protective duties, effect of, 65.
Public works, 109.

QUICKSILVER. *See* Mercury.

RAILWAYS, capital in, 22, 30, 48.
—— cost per mile, 167.
—— goods tariff, 49.

INDEX.

Railways, men employed in, 115.
— of all nations, 47, 167.
— of Great Britain, 50.
— passenger fares, 49.
— steam-power on, 52.
— traffic of, 167.
Raisins, consumption of, 176.
— price of, 180, 186.
Reaping-machine, 145, 146.
Regenerator, Cowper's, 73.
Rental. *See* Houses.
Rice, consumption, 176.
— price, 180, 184, 186.
River Plate, cattle, 83, 173.
— exports to, 104.
— wool of, 60.
Roads and bridges, 30.
Roumania, cattle, 83, 173.
— debt, 163.
— grain, 80.
— population, 96.
Rum, price of, 180, 186.
Russia, agriculture, 80, 84, 171.
— banking, 160.
— books, 69.
— capital invested, 22.
— cattle, 173.
— coinage, 16, 157.
— commerce, 35, 164.
— cost of industry, 55.
— debt, 30, 163.
— earnings, 30, 112.
— energy, 53.
— finances, 26, 162.
— food-supply, 86, 92, 175.
— gold production, 13, 158.
— import dues, 37.
— iron and steel, 64.
— liquor, 175.
— living, cost of, 113.
— manufactures, 168.
— military, 28.
— mining, 73, 76.
— population, 96.
— railways, 47, 167.
— shipping, 166.

Russia, steam-power, 53.
— sugar crop, 174.
— summary, industrial, 115.
— taxation, 30, 162.
— telegraphs, 50.
— timber, 67.
— tobacco, 174.
— trade with Great Britain, 142.
— vineyards, 172.
— wages, 125, 132.
— wealth, 30, 110.
Russo-Turkish war, 30.
Rye crop of the world, 80.

SADOWA campaign, 148.
Sailcloth, price of, 182, 186.
Salt, consumption, 92.
— duties, 99.
— price, 182, 186.
Saltpetre, price of, 180, 186.
Santo Domingo currency, 137.
Savings. *See* Accumulation.
Savings banks, 23, 143, 147, 161.
Savoy, annexation of, 147.
Scandinavia, agriculture, 80, 84, 173.
— banking, 160.
— books and paper, 69.
— coin, 16, 157.
— commerce, 35, 164.
— cost of industry, 55.
— death-rate, 99.
— debt, 30.
— earnings, 30.
— emigration, 101.
— energy, 53.
— finances, 26.
— food-supply, 86, 92, 175.
— import dues, 37.
— living, cost of, 113.
— railways, 47, 167.
— steam-power, 53.
— summary, industrial, 115.
— telegraphs, 50.
— trade with Great Britain, 142.
— wages, 125, 132.

INDEX.

Scandinavia, wealth, 30.
—— *See* Sweden, Denmark.
Scheldt dues abolished, 148.
Scotland, agriculture, 172.
—— emigration, 102.
—— population, 96.
—— wealth, 111.
—— *See* Great Britain.
Seamen of all nations, 115.
Seamen, British, 42.
Seed-clover, price of, 180, 186.
Senior on prices, 189.
Serfs, Russian, emancipated, 30, 147.
Servia, debt, 163.
—— population, 96.
Sexes of emigrants, 101.
Sheep, price of, 180, 186.
—— *See* Cattle.
Shepherds' wages, 131.
Shipbuilding, 66, 165.
Shipping of all flags, 41, 166.
—— effect on prices, 45.
Sickness, days of, 99.
Siemens steel, 64, 119.
Silk industry, 168.
—— price, 180, 186.
Silks, price of, 182, 186.
—— value of, 122.
Silver, stock of, 11, 158.
—— price of, 12, 145.
Sleswig-Holstein annexed, 148.
Smith, Adam, on prices, 189.
Soap, price of, 182, 186.
Sœtbeer's price-level, 188.
Sound-dues abolished, 146.
Spain, agriculture, 80, 84, 171.
—— banking, 160.
—— books, 69.
—— coinage, 16, 157.
—— commerce, 35, 164.
—— cost of industry, 55.
—— debt, 30, 163.
—— earnings, 30, 112.
—— emigration, 101.
—— energy, 53.
—— finances, 26, 162.

Spain, food-supply, 86, 92, 175.
—— import-dues, 37.
—— investments, new, 22.
—— liquor, 175.
—— living, cost of, 113.
—— manufactures, 168.
—— military, 28.
—— mining, 74, 76.
—— population, 96.
—— railways, 47, 167.
—— shipping, 43, 166.
—— steam-power, 53.
—— summary, industrial, 115.
—— taxation, 30.
—— telegraphs, 50.
—— trade with Great Britain, 142.
—— vineyards, 172.
—— wages, 126.
—— wealth, 30, 110.
—— wine, price of, 121.
Specie payments, United States, 151.
Spinner. *See* Cotton-spinner.
Spirits, consumption, 175.
—— price, 182, 186.
—— value, 117.
Steam, effect on prices, 135.
Steam-ploughs, use of, 144.
Steam-power of nations, 53.
Steamers of all flags, 42, 52.
Steel industry, 65, 119, 148.
—— price, 182, 186.
Straits Settlements, trade, &c., 103.
Strikes of workmen, 149, 150.
Suez Canal, 4, 149, 165.
Sugar, consumption, 92, 143, 176.
—— price, 121, 130, 180, 186.
—— production, 94, 174.
—— transport, 35.
—— value, 122, 177.
Summary of industries, 115.
Sweden, agriculture, 84, 173.
—— cattle, 173.
—— debt, 163.
—— earnings, 112.

INDEX.

Sweden, finances, 162.
—— food-supply, 87, 92, 175.
—— iron industry, 64.
—— liquor, 175.
—— military, 28.
—— mining, 73, 76.
—— population, 96.
—— railways, 47, 167.
—— shipping, 43, 166.
—— wealth, 110.
—— See Scandinavia.
Switzerland, banking, 160.
—— books, 69.
—— earnings, 112.
—— emigration, 101.
—— population, 96.
—— railways, 47, 167.
—— wealth, 110.

TALLOW, price of, 130, 180, 186.
Tariffs, British and United States, 38, 164.
Taxation of nations, 26, 30, 113.
—— local, 31.
Tea, consumption, 143, 175.
—— price, 121, 180, 186.
—— production, 94.
—— value, 122.
Telegraphs, purchase of, 149.
—— of all nations, 50.
Telephone invented, 150.
Thiers, fall of, 149.
Timber, consumption, 67.
—— price, 120, 130, 180, 186.
—— production, 67.
—— value, 122, 177.
Tin industry, 75.
—— price, 1·2, 186.
Tobacco, consumption, 175.
—— price, 121, 180, 184.
—— production, 94, 174.
—— value, 122.
Tooke, opinions of, 135, 189.
Toronto house-building, 109.
Trade, balance of, 36, 164.
—— British, 36, 139, 142, 164.

Trade of nations, 34, 164.
Traffic of railways, 167.
—— British lines, 50.
Transport. See Freight, Carrying-trade.
Treaty, Cobden's, 4, 147.
Tunis, annexation of, 151.
Turin, house-building, 109.
Turkey, debt of, 163.
Turnips, area under, 172.

UNITED STATES, agriculture, 80, 84, 171.
—— banking, 23, 160.
—— bankruptcy returns, 24.
—— books and paper, 69.
—— capital invested, 22.
—— cattle, 83, 173.
—— Clearing-Houses, 160.
—— coal statistics, 72.
—— coinage, 16, 157.
—— commerce, 35, 38, 164.
—— cost of industry, 55.
—— cotton crop, 59.
—— death-rate, 99.
—— debt, 30, 148, 151, 163.
—— earnings, 30, 112.
—— emigration to, 101.
—— energy, 53.
—— finances, 26, 162.
—— food-supply, 86, 92, 175.
—— gold, current of, 15, 157.
—— —— production, 13, 71, 159.
—— import-dues, 37, 164.
—— iron, 64.
—— leather, 68.
—— liquor, 175.
—— living, cost of, 113.
—— manufactures, 64, 168.
—— military, 29.
—— mining, 73, 76.
—— petroleum, 76.
—— population, 96.
—— price-levels, 6, 155.
—— price-list, 183.
—— railways, 47, 167.

INDEX.

United States savings-banks, 160.
—— shipbuilding, 66.
—— shipping, 43, 165.
—— silver, 13, 15.
—— steam-power, 52.
—— steel, 65.
—— summary, industrial, 115.
—— taxation, 30.
—— telegraphs, 50.
—— timber, 67.
—— tobacco, 174.
—— trade with Great Britain, 38, 142.
—— vineyards, 172.
—— wages, 126, 128, 133.
—— war, cost of, 30.
—— wealth, 30, 110.
—— wool-clip, 60.
Uruguay, republic of, 84.

Vienna Clearing-House, 160.
—— crisis, 149.
Vineyards of all nations, 172.

Wages and cost of food, 126, 132.
—— and product of labour, 133.
—— in various countries, 124, 126.
—— in Great Britain, 125, 132.
—— M'Culloch on, 189.
—— Tooke on, 189, 190.
Wars, cost of, 30.
—— effects of, 3, 59, 130, 134.
—— various, 147–152.
Washington, silver at, 14.
Waterloo, effect on prices, 130.
Wealth of nations, 30, 110.
—— increase of, 142.

Wear and tear of gold, 158.
Wells, oil, 76.
West Indies, coffee, 173.
—— debt, 104.
—— population, 103.
—— sugar, 174.
—— tobacco, 174.
—— trade, 103.
Wheat, consumption, 143.
—— crop of the world, 80.
—— price, 118, 130, 180, 184.
—— supply of Great Britain, 88.
Wine, consumption, 175.
—— price, 121, 180, 186.
—— production, 172.
—— value, 122.
Wire, price of, 182, 186.
Wood, price of, 180, 186.
—— *See* Timber.
Wool, carried over sea, 35.
—— consumption, 58, 62.
—— price, 120, 130, 180, 184.
—— production, 60.
—— value, 122, 177.
Woollens, manufacture, 170.
—— price, 120, 182.
—— value, 122, 177.
Work. *See* Energy, Labour.
Works. *See* Public Works.
Workmen's wages, 126, 132.
—— average product, 81, 128.
Worsted stuffs, 182, 186.

Yarn, price of, 182, 186.

Zinc, industry, 75.
—— price, 182, 186.

A. M. D. G.

OPINIONS ON THE AUTHOR'S WORKS.

"They are the quintessence of statistics."—*Leroy-Beaulieu.*

"Display a vast amount of research."—*Times.*

"Deserve the highest praise."—*Emile de Laveleye.*

"Remarkably well arranged and clear."—*Economist.*

"Inexhaustible treasury of facts."—*Economiste Français.*

"Books of reference as trustworthy as they are unique."—*Scotsman.*

"Written with great care and intelligence."—*New York Nation.*

"Clear, accurate, and comprehensive."—*Toronto Globe.*

"Useful and interesting."—*Statistical Journal.*

"Most original and intelligible of all works on statistics."—*Academy.*

"A boon to the student or public writer."—*Irish Times.*

"Compiled in a convenient and easily intelligible form."—*Spectator.*

"As useful as the Census Report."—*Graphic.*

"No books of reference have higher claims."—*Globe.*

"They are a mine of facts."—*Weekly Register.*

"Often quoted as an authority."—*United States Census Report.*

"Bring a vast number of facts within small compass."—*Daily News.*

www.ingramcontent.com/pod-product-compliance
Lightning Source LLC
Chambersburg PA
CBHW021834230426
43669CB00008B/963